# SNOOK ON A FLY

# SNOOK ON A FLY

*Tackle, Tactics, and Tips for Catching the Great Saltwater Gamefish*

NORM ZEIGLER

STACKPOLE
BOOKS

Published by
STACKPOLE BOOKS
5067 Ritter Road
Mechanicsburg, PA 17055
www.stackpolebooks.com

Printed in China

First edition

10  9  8  7  6  5  4  3  2  1

*Photographs by Norm Zeigler, except where otherwise noted*
*Illustrations by Dave Hall*

**Library of Congress Cataloging-in-Publication Data**

Zeigler, Norm.
    Snook on a fly : tackle, tactics, and tips for catching the great saltwater game-fish / Norm Zeigler.
        p. cm.
    Includes bibliographical references and index.
    ISBN-13: 978-0-8117-0201-0
    ISBN-10: 0-8117-0201-4
    1. Snook fishing. 2. Saltwater fly fishing. I. Title.

SH691.S64Z45 2007
799.1'772—dc22
                                        2006013885

*This book is for my father,*
*Norman F. Zeigler,*
*who taught me to love clean waters*
*and wild places.*

# CONTENTS

# A Few Words About Those Snuke

A funny-looking name, as fish names go: snook. These days most anglers pronounce it like "cook" or "chinook." But deep in the mangrove wilds of southern Florida, you'll still find some old-timers who talk about fishing for "snuke."

That variable vowel often rides on an out-thrust lower jaw, curiously reminiscent of *Centropomus* morphology. This, among other mannerisms (such as wearing long sleeves in 95-degree heat), distinguishes the veteran snuker from the uncautious outsider, who immediately identifies himself as such by asking about "those snuke."

Snook or snuke—for those of us who've quietly been pursuing this magical fish with fly rods for years, Norm Zeigler's book serves as a refreshing piece of affirmation. Have you often thought of snook as the ultimate "fly fish"? You're not alone. They strike hard; they run far; they jump high. They are a marvel to look at, with those glittering scales, golden fins, single black stripe and gaping, underslung mouth. They also confound us with a selectivity which at times brings to mind that of spring creek brown trout.

For those unfamiliar with the species, *Snook on a Fly* contains everything you need to get started—including inspiration. Wearing his wading boots and fishing vest, Norm steps deftly between roles as informed narrator and consummate fishing buddy. He takes us wading on cold winter afternoons, hunting shadows on blinding white beach sands and navigating the mangrove labyrinth of southwest Florida.

Through personal anecdotes and interviews with experts in the field, Norm offers an up-close look at the surprising habits of *Centropomus undecimalis,* the common snook. As strong a tactician as any writer in fly fishing, he appropriately demystifies rigging, fly selection, and casting techniques. Once you understand the seasonal and tidal movements of this tropical species, and its ambush feeding style, fly-fishing for snook is mostly a simple affair. A modest-priced rod and reel, a basic leader, a handful of flies, a vacant stretch of shoreline, and you're snook fishing. Or snuke fishing.

There is another audience this book will surely speak to, and that is the legion of anglers who've long fished for snook with natural bait, jigs, or plugs on spinning or bait-casting tackle. For a fish that routinely scales 10 pounds or more, snook at times focus on very tiny prey—miniscule baitfish and shrimp, items impractical to duplicate, let alone cast, with conventional tackle.

Dedicated fly fishermen love snook for the various challenges the species offers, and the special beauty of its habitat. But stepping beyond aesthetics, fly fishing is a downright effective mode for catching snook. Whether you're reading this as a lifelong fly fisherman, a complete novice, or a light-tackle angler looking to round out your arsenal, *Snook on a Fly* has something for you.

Jeff Weakley
Editor, *Florida Sportsman* magazine

# ACKNOWLEDGMENTS

I am indebted to many good friends and colleagues who helped transform this project from an intriguing idea into a book. I owe special thanks to Bill Tapply, Nelson Bryant, Berris Samples, and Jerry Kustich for their friendship, encouragement, and professional advice. Ron Taylor at the Florida Marine Research Institute generously shared his time and knowledge to help me understand the complexities of snook biology, as did Professor Ernst Peebles of the University of South Florida, Dr. William N. Eschmeyer at the Department of Ichthyology of the California Academy of Sciences, and Dr. Jose Leal of the Bailey-Matthews Shell Museum on Sanibel Island. As always, my agent, Peter Rubie of the Peter Rubie Literary Agency, contributed his literary expertise and business acumen.

My longtime fly-fishing pals Dick White, Dave Ford, Jim Baldwin, Dave Schwerdt, Bill Higgins, Steve Bailey, and Dave Gibson contributed by sharing the excitement and magic of snook fishing in all seasons and many places—from mangrove shorelines to beaches, bayous, grass flats, and ditches near and far.

Ralph Woodring and Robin Ramming at the Bait Box on Sanibel Island and Mike McComas at Lee Island Outfitters in Fort Myers were generous in supplying equipment for some of the photographs. Dave Westra at Lehr's Economy Tackle in North Fort Myers supplied salient advice, as did the staff at Bait-N-Wait in Fort Myers Beach.

Most important, of course, are the love and support of my family: my children, Travis and Katrina, and my wife, Libby Grimm.

# INTRODUCTION

One of the great things about fly fishing is its endless variety. But like devotees of many other pastimes, we fly fishers sometimes become so comfortable staying within familiar parameters that we miss out on new and exhilarating possibilities.

Like many other anglers, my formative fly-fishing years were spent largely in pursuit of trout. While teaching myself tactics and techniques through a combination of reading, research, and trial and error, I wandered in search of any and all varieties of these exquisite salmonids on rivers, lakes, and streams from Maine to Vancouver Island and many places in between. Later, during fifteen years spent living and working in Europe, I sought them (and their distant cousins, grayling) from Denmark to Spain and from the Scottish Highlands to the High Tatra. In those years, the mountains, the cold, clear waters, and their numinous, brilliantly colored fish—brook trout, browns, rainbows, cutthroats, and their myriad sub-groups near and far—seemed world enough for anyone's angling lifetime. I knew that I could never tire of them. And I never have.

But in 1994, confronting a personal health crisis that prompted one doctor to prescribe "somewhere where there is no winter and the air is clean," I moved with my family to southwest Florida. At first, the sense of loss was grievous. I spent so much time wondering whether I would ever again wade a trout stream that I could not see the wonders of the whole new fly-fishing world that awaited my discovery. But finally, during long, slow years of treatment and recuperation, I began to get a glimpse of it. And it was pure magic. A big part of that magic was a powerful, bronze-backed, silver-sided fish with an elegant black stripe tracing the graceful curve of its lateral line from gill slit to tail fork.

This book is about my love affair with snook, wherever they may be— from tangled mangrove shorelines to white-sand beaches, from the tranquil waters of roadside ditches to the fast-rushing tidal currents of cuts, creeks, and passes. In these pages, readers will learn how to find and catch these gleaming, rocket-powered aerialists, which may be saltwater fly fishing's most intriguing inshore gamefish. Snook are as wily and mystifying as bonefish, and as electrifying on the end of a fly line as silver lightning. In addition to providing details of equipment, techniques, and biology, this book seeks to convey the magic and mystery inherent in the quest for these stunningly beautiful, tough, graceful, hard-fighting fish that have dominated my fly fishing for more than a decade.

The allure of snook is far reaching. From Oregon to Arkansas, Montana to Maine, Illinois to Bavaria, and many places in between, I have found fly fishers of all stripes who are fascinated by snook. Whether these would-be snookers are encountered on rivers, streams, oceans, lakes or at presentations, social gatherings, or club events, the fascination manifests itself in piqued curiosity, keen queries, and a subtle yearning that inflects body language, phraseology, and voice timbre. The fascination extends across the angling spectrum, from once-a-year vacation anglers to dedicated, near-daily aficionados; from dyed-in-the-wool Appalachian brook trouters to Great Lakes walleye devotees, midwesterners weaned on largemouths, New England striper enthusiasts, Northwest steelheaders, and even Bahamas bonefish addicts. Additionally, the idea of fly fishing for snook intrigues (and sometimes intimidates) many spin fishers and bait casters who have pursued them for years with jigs, plugs, spinners, spoons, and bait. For those of us fortunate enough to fish for snook on flies, fascination quickly becomes infatuation.

No fishing book can be all things to all anglers, but this one was written with two goals in mind: (1) to provide basic information and instruction for neophytes so that they can quickly and effortlessly become successful snookers, and (2) to offer advanced tips and techniques for experienced snookers seeking to enhance their knowledge and skills. I hope it will also inspire, entertain, and enlighten fly fishers and aspiring fly fishers who have pursued or dreamed of pursuing these magnificent creatures.

Because I am not presumptuous enough to think that I know everything about fly fishing for snook, I have consulted experts in many aspects of the sport to augment my own judgments, perspectives, and experiences. These include guides, marine biologists, and other passionate anglers.

# CHAPTER 1

# *Why Snook?*

They glide across the shallows like ghostly, silver-gray shadows, occasionally singly, sometimes in twos and threes, but mostly in elongated schools of a dozen or more. Some of the schools are huge—thirty, forty, half a hundred fish stretched out for 50 feet or more.

Swimming close in along the beach, they follow a straight course, westward with the longshore current. This day, with a light east wind riffling the Gulf, they are more confident, less spooky than usual, cruising at walking speed up the shoreline. Occasionally, just occasionally, one strays from the course to chase a baitfish or inspect a movement on the bottom.

The next group, two dozen fish moving in an elongated ellipse, is already in sight. Facing east, I make two false casts, shoot the line, and drop my Schminnow two feet in front of the lead fish. I strip once, twice; the fish surges forward, grabs the fly, and, when I set the hook with a sharp, straight pull on the line, takes off back down the shore in a rush. When I raise the rod tip, the fish leaps clear of the water, shaking its head and tailwalking for a second before falling back.

After three healthy runs and five jumps, the fish is finally spent and turns on its side in the shallows, a leader's length from shore. I raise the rod above my head, ease in the fish, and stick my thumb in its mouth, gripping its lower jaw between thumb and forefinger. In a couple of seconds I have gently backed the hook out of the corner of its jaw. I kneel down in the sandy shallows, letting the fish grip my thumb in its mouth

1

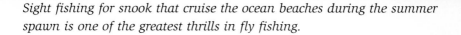

*Sight fishing for snook that cruise the ocean beaches during the summer spawn is one of the greatest thrills in fly fishing.*

and moving it back and forth to pass water over its gills. In less than half a minute the fish releases my thumb, turns seaward with a swish of its tail, and slowly swims out to deeper water.

Stepping back onto the beach, I move back 10 feet from the water's edge. In a practiced, automatic sequence, I quickly inspect the fly, slide my fingers along the lower end of the bite tippet to check for abrasion, then glance down the beach to get ready for the next school.

One of the favorite quarries of the old New England whalers was the right whale, so named because its physical and behavioral traits were ideally suited—"right"—for their needs. For saltwater fly fishers, you could say that the snook is the "right fish." Some fly anglers—especially those who regard tarpon as mere flashy genetic giants—consider snook the tropics' and subtropics' premier inshore gamefish.

Snook are extremely wary but aggressive feeders and fierce fighters. Seatrout are flashier to look at but weaker fighters. Redfish pack a wallop but lack snook's spectacular aerialist antics. And unlike tarpon, snook are delicious to eat.

The genus and species designation for the common snook, *Centropomus undecimalis,* was chosen by German researcher Marcus Elieser Bloch in 1792. *Centropomus* is a combination of the Greek words for "stinging cover" and refers to the fish's hard, sharp gill plate, or operculum. *Undecimalis* derives from the Latin root word *undecim,* or "eleven," and indicates the number of rays in the snook's posterior dorsal fin. Genetically, snook are unique; they are the only member of their genus in the Atlantic Ocean.

The name snook comes from the Dutch word *snoek,* meaning "pike." Other common appellations include robalo, ravillia, linesides, linesider, and sergeant fish. But whatever they are called, snook are easy to love, especially for fly fishers. They are beautiful, impulsive, and elusive. They are wily, powerful quarry that fight as fiercely as striped bass and jump like rainbow trout on steroids. If redfish are the fullbacks of inshore saltwater fly fishing—bull-necked and doggedly powerful—snook are the wide receivers—streamlined, muscular, and leapingly fleet.

A lot of fly fishers who have never fished for snook know a little bit about them. They may have read about them, heard tales from friends and acquaintances who have fished for them, or watched one of television's celebrity fly fishers pursue them. But as is the case with anything experienced vicariously, this is a dry and detached knowledge; it may not be inaccurate, but it is certainly incomplete. Like love, the only way to truly understand it is to experience it.

*The best beach fishing for snook occurs on days when a light breeze riffles the water's surface, making the fish less spooky.*

It is difficult to exaggerate the passion sparked by these "mere" fish. Captain Ray Van Horn, originally from South Carolina but now living and guiding in Tarpon Springs, Florida, is a nationally ranked tournament bass, tarpon, and redfish angler. He has fished for most of the saltwater and freshwater gamefish in the United States and is not exactly a touchy-feely type. But when it comes to snook, Van Horn is not shy about showing his sentimental side. "I could never live anywhere where there aren't any snook," he says. It is a common outlook.

My philosophy on target species and regions tends to run along the lines of a verse from a 1970s song: "If you can't be with the one you love, then love the one you're with." In tiny mountain streams I love 6-inch brook trout. In farm ponds I love sunfish. On Cape Cod I love striped bass. But there are some angling love affairs that are worth a bit of extra effort to foster and sustain.

There are many reasons for fly rodders to love snook. One of the most compelling is their morphology—specifically, their size and body structure. In my experience, the majority of snook caught are between 20 and 28 inches. These are not stylishly svelte, capriciously swift, low-endurance creatures like Spanish mackerel or shad. They are muscular, thick-shouldered, high-stamina, piscine torpedoes that put a bend in any outfit lighter than a 10-weight and keep battling relentlessly to the shore (or boat) and beyond. Closely linked to snook's physiology is their fighting ability. And what fighters they are! On tackle suited to their size, multiple long runs and jumps are common.

It is their aerial antics that really set snook apart from other top-rate gamefish. I have never had a redfish jump. The same goes for bonefish. Seatrout jump occasionally, and Spanish mackerel, striped bass, bluefish, jack crevalle, and other saltwater species become airborne on rare occasions. But when they are hooked, snook like to "get some air." Their jumps vary from thrashing, gill-rattling tarpon impersonations to cartwheels, rocketlike vertical explosions, and greyhounding forward leaps. On more than a few occasions, a sore arm or shoulder, not a halt in the action, has put an end to my snook fishing. This is the kind of discomfort and fatigue that all fly fishers long to experience more of.

Another reason to love snook is their style, elegance, and beauty. There is no denying that, because of their fighting ability, bonefish are superb fly-fishing quarry. But compared with the elegantly proportioned snook, a bonefish—with its chinless, comically underdeveloped lower jaw,

*One characteristic that sets snook apart from other saltwater fly-rod quarry is their spectacular aerialist antics.*

blunt wedge of a snout, and small, bottom-situated mouth—looks like a glorified sucker.

Trim but well-muscled, sleek but not skinny, with subtly coordinated color tones, highlights, and accents that are pleasing to the eye but not gaudy (compare peacock bass or roosterfish), snook are among the most attractive of fish: white marble belly; gleaming silver sides; dark, greenish gold back; fins a translucent gold tipped with brown; firm black stripe accentuating the lateral line. They could have been designed by a talented marine architect with a specialty in functional design and an extra flair for style. Like evening wear at the opera, a snook's colors catch but do not assault the eye.

It may be fatuous to anthropomorphize a fish, but with their under-slung jaws and defiant, pouting lower lips, snook seem to exude an insouciant confidence, even a swagger. When they move through the water and jump, it is with power, subtle grace, and economy of motion. From their streamlined, faintly upswept prow of a nose to their tapered and gently curving tail fork, they are a fish that everyone is proud to be seen with.

Ronald Taylor, a fisheries biologist at the Florida Marine Research Institute in St. Petersburg, who has studied and fished for snook for more than twenty years, states it more succinctly: "It's the most elegant fish in the water, an icon."

Yet another agreeable attribute of linesiders is their dependability. Unlike the saltwater pelagic species, such as striped bass, bluefish, bonito, and Spanish mackerel, snook are not fickle, seasonal visitors but reliable, year-round residents. Throughout their range, they can be caught in good numbers every season of the year. And they can be caught from shore, while wading, or from a boat.

One of the greatest thrills in snook angling is sight fishing them in clear, shallow water along mainland beaches, barrier islands, and sand flats. It easily rivals—and, in my opinion, surpasses—the closest comparable saltwater fly-fishing pursuit: bonefishing. Curiously, for a variety of reasons (poorly researched magazine articles, guides with limited firsthand knowledge, and one-dimensional television shows), this aspect of the sport is largely absent from the public consciousness. Even some experienced snook anglers tend to regard beach sight fishing as a serendipitous anomaly that presents itself only rarely and under limited meteorological and

*Ron Taylor, a researcher at the Florida Marine Research Institute, calls snook "the most elegant fish in the water."*

hydrographic conditions. The truth is that in many places, good, sandy shoreline sight fishing is available periodically during nearly half the year—from mid-April to early October—reaching its peak during the summer months. The few knowledgeable fly anglers who discover this heart-racing pastime quickly become hard-core addicts.

In one sense, fly fishing for snook is simple. Unlike the pursuit of other marquee saltwater species—dolphin, tarpon, king mackerel—it does not require a boat or elaborate ancillary equipment. For snookers, more gear does not necessarily mean more fish, and certainly not more enjoyment. Henry David Thoreau, one of our great American naturalists and writers (and also an avid angler), espoused a life tenet that many snook anglers would do well to heed: "Simplify, simplify."

Contrary to some industry advertising, $30,000 flats boats equipped with fish finders, GPS, trolling motors, push poles, and poling platforms are not essential or de rigueur. They do increase anglers' range and options, but the flip side of the coin is that I have watched many high-powered, top-of-the-line craft run past excellent snook waters at top speed in a frantic race for some distant snook angling nirvana. Many of the best spots are easily reached without a boat by wading from shore.

Marshall Cutchin, legendary Key West guide and publisher of the online fly-fishing magazine *midcurrent.com*, calls snook "a unique fish because they're both a flats fish and not a flats fish. You can catch them in 6 inches of water and then in 10 feet of water."

For fly fishers, the clincher in their progression to total snook infatuation is usually the realization that these highly efficient marine predators love flies—all kinds of flies: streamers, poppers, jig flies, spoon flies, gurglers, and sliders; white, brown, black, red, yellow, chartreuse, and endless combinations thereof; along mangrove shorelines, on shallow grass flats, over oyster bars, in potholes, in channels, and on the beach. Snook do not take flies cautiously and reluctantly or only occasionally, when there is little else available. They eat them like a chocoholic devours fudge, like a kid at a movie wolfs down popcorn. The main reason for this behavior is that snook are ambush predators, not scavengers. They prefer their prey alive, and their feeding response is triggered more by movement, color, and (occasionally) sound than by smell. They will swim right past a hunk of dead bait to slam a Deceiver or a Schminnow.

Many a day I have caught cruising snook that have swum a gauntlet of freshly thawed shrimp or cut mullet proffered by sand-spike bottom fishermen just yards away. It is always satisfying to be able to provide such firsthand instruction to fellow anglers, especially those who view fly fishing as a bafflingly arcane, self-imposed handicap. There is nothing like success to pique people's interest and bring new fly fishers into the sport.

The fact that snook fillets are a delicacy is a negligible consideration for most fly fishers. Like freshwater trout, they are too valuable and magnificent a gamefish to routinely harvest, and most of us release almost all we land. However, I am not a catch-and-release fanatic, and once every year or two I do keep a snook. Their mild, flaky white flesh is among the most delicious seafood in the world.

A side benefit of fishing for snook is that it takes anglers to areas with good populations of other excellent fly-rod quarry. Most common are redfish and seatrout, but other species caught both incidentally and in good numbers along with snook include Spanish mackerel, ladyfish, baby tarpon, jack crevalle, sheepshead, and mangrove snapper.

*A grinning Dave Schwerdt holds a 27-inch snook he caught while wading the edge of a grass flat. Because snook are predominantly a shallow-water species, a boat is unnecessary in many places.*

My friend Dennis Cannizzaro, a snowbird who migrates between upstate New York and Fort Myers, loves south Florida's amazing variety of fish. But when asked to choose his number one, he does not hesitate. "Snook are fabulous," he says. "They're my favorite. Because they fight so hard on the rod, and they jump."

To paraphrase Will Rogers, I never met a fish I did not like. But in the two main areas of my fly-fishing life—salt water and fresh water—there are distinct favorites. In fresh water it is trout. In the salt it is snook. None of the others comes close. Even Taylor, who prides himself on being a dispassionate scientist, cannot help waxing poetic about fishing for snook: "At that moment when you have it on the end of your line, you transcend time and space." And whether you fish for them on white-sand beaches or in gnarly mangrove swamps, snook take you to some fascinating and stunning areas that are rich in wildlife and every bit as beautiful as a clear trout stream in the Rockies.

# CHAPTER 2

# *A Snook's Life Story*

The key to finding and catching snook is understanding their life cycle and behavior patterns. As with many fish, a snook's life cycle is both complex and simple, equal parts mystery and practical biology. The two most telling factors are these: First, they are a shallow-water, inshore species and spend their lives in estuaries, on grass flats, and close in along the beaches. Offshore catches are rare and usually incidental. Second, they are heat seekers; it is virtually impossible for the water to be too warm for them. In summer—their most active season—they thrive in water temperatures from the high 80s to low 90s. The obverse also applies. They will do whatever is necessary to avoid cold. When the water temperature drops into the mid-60s, they go off their feed, sometimes into semi-dormancy. If it gets below 50, they begin to die.

Befitting their physiology, life for all snook begins in the warm months. In a ritual as old as the species, large, egg-carrying females and the smaller males meet up along beaches and in passes, generally from April to the end of October. As with many creatures, successful propagation is partly a matter of incredible reproductive fecundity. A single adult snook is literally one in a million, or more. Snook are living confirmation of the cliché that nature is careless of the individual but careful of the species. The number of individual organisms involved in the early stages of the reproductive cycle is staggering. But the survival odds they face are daunting.

Like most other fish species, snook do not mate or pair up. The do not construct nests, redds, or spawning beds. They reproduce by so-called

10

broadcast spawning, with males and females ejecting free-floating sperm and eggs into the water simultaneously and in close proximity. Scientist Ronald Taylor, at the Florida Marine Research Institute in St. Petersburg, found that spawning females release up to 1.25 million eggs at a time. Research has shown that, under laboratory conditions, close to 90 percent of the eggs are fertilized, although Taylor speculates that success rates are lower in the open ocean. Despite their numbers, these eggs are a fragile link in the species' survival, vulnerable to myriad predators and the whims of nature. "You can brush an egg with your hand or with a feather in a beaker of water and crush it," Taylor says. "Think of the turbulence that is caused in an open ocean environment by wind and wave action. . . . Then think of things in terms of red tide or anoxic water or hydrogen sulfide."

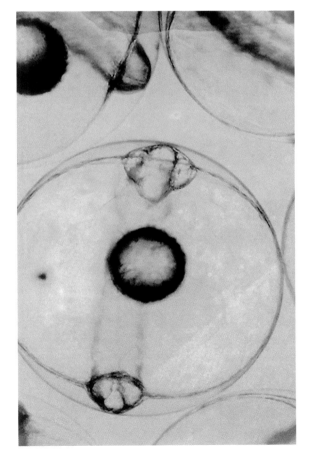

*Fertilized snook eggs are so fragile that they can be damaged by a feather.* FLORIDA MARINE RESEARCH INSTITUTE

In his presentations and research writings, Taylor is careful to advise that developmental variations are common among all fish species. And this certainly holds true for the snook's life history: their size, maturation, and age ratios vary within certain ranges. But the developmental process does follow a general pattern, beginning with the eggs released in passes and along summer shorelines.

The eggs are minuscule, between 0.024 and 0.031 inches in diameter. Once fertilized, they become embryos and, about a day later, hatch into larvae. Unless he or she were a marine biologist, a person viewing a snook larva would be unlikely to recognize it. These free-floating zooplankton, about 0.055 inch long, are nearly transparent, with no mouth, a tiny blob of oil under the head, and a yolk sac hanging down like a pot belly. They look about as much like an adult snook as a bottom-crawling nymph resembles a wispy-winged adult mayfly.

By late in the second day of its life, the larva has increased its length 50 percent (to about 0.084 inch), and the oil drop and yolk sac begin to shrink. Another day brings color to its eyes, a working mouth, and the development of a rudimentary digestive tract. The larva begins to eat microplankton, no longer relying only on the yolk sac for nourishment. By four days old, the larva is recognizable as a fish, although its features remain generic. A few more days bring about jaw development and an increase in length to about 0.2 inch. Teeth and hardening of the jawbone come with the next growth spurt, to 0.3 inch. It is still too tiny to go its own way, subject largely to the whims of tides and currents.

After another two weeks of aimless drifting and feeding on plankton—a period of continuous growth and development—the larva has finally become a juvenile. Despite being barely an inch long, it now looks like a snook, right down to the prognathous lower jaw and distinctive black stripe. The little fish, once a helpless microscopic organism, is no longer merely buffeted and battered by fickle waters, forced to go with the flow. Finally it can seek its own direction and destination. Of course, it does not consciously "decide" where to go, but driven by powerful instincts and species memory, it follows a primordial urge to fulfill two paramount survival needs: food and safety.

The ideal place—providing safe haven and commissary in one—is a mangrove estuary. In many areas, mangroves are as essential to healthy snook populations as cold, clear, moving water is to trout. Where there are no mangroves, there are no snook—or at least not in appreciable num-

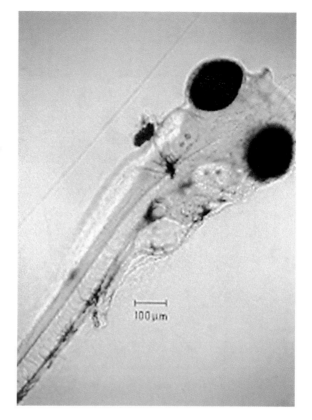

*Only a trained marine biologist would be likely to recognize a neonatal snook larva.*

FLORIDA MARINE RESEARCH

INSTITUTE

bers. Healthy snook populations exist only where there are healthy, abundant mangroves. And if mangrove habitats are damaged or destroyed, snook populations soon follow. In areas with few mangrove estuaries, such as parts of Florida's Atlantic coast, freshwater creeks, salt marshes, and structured waterways (canals with riprap and pilings) provide juvenile snook nurseries, but they are much less productive than the abundant, phenomenally fecund mangrove habitats of the southern Gulf shore.

The tiny snook, still no bigger than the minnows it will later feed on, is drawn to the mangroves like a butterfly to a blossom. For a juvenile snook, it is a great place to grow up. Among tangled, barnacle-encrusted roots, oyster clusters, overhanging branches, organic detritus, and complex benthic communities, it finds cover, shade, abundant food sources, and clean, warm water. For the next six months or longer, life is a matter of hide and eat for the little snook. With its virtually insatiable appetite, it grows very fast. At first it consumes zooplankton as well as tiny shrimp-

*Once it reaches the juvenile stage, a snook is a miniature version of an adult fish.* DAVE JENKINS, MOTE MARINE LABORATORY

like creatures called copepods and microcrustaceans. Occasionally it supplements its diet with insects.

During this time, nature's age-old survival struggle—to eat and not be eaten—never ceases. Our little juvenile must constantly dodge a plethora of predators. Among the avian variety, snook's enemies include wading birds such as ibises, herons, egrets, storks, and bitterns; raptors such as ospreys and eagles; and swimming and diving birds such as anhingas, loons, and cormorants. Any larger piscivorous fish is also a deadly threat. A juvenile snook must fear and avoid some of its most common co-inhabitants of the mangroves, especially ladyfish, seatrout, redfish, needlefish, mangrove snappers, largemouth bass (in freshwater upstream habitats), and even its own cannibalistic older cousins. Reptiles—alligators, turtles, and water snakes—play a comparatively small role in snook predation, but they also take their toll.

Although age, size, and maturation ratios vary, month after month of ravenous feeding brings explosive growth for the juvenile snook. At one month it may be just over 2 inches long, at three months about 4 inches, at six months 10 inches, and at nine months 15 inches. With greater size comes a graduation to a more substantial diet of larger prey: common shrimp, small crabs, and fish. Snook love to eat fish most of all.

One year after it was hatched, the snook is still a juvenile, unable to reproduce. It does not join the sexually mature adults in their annual migration to the spawning grounds; instead, it remains in the sheltered estuary. Given the timing of the spawning season, the final maturation to adulthood for our snook likely occurs in the cooler months—November through April—during its second year of life. At this point, depending on its growth rate, the fish is generally between 14 and 19 inches long. Like the majority of its coevals, this snook is male.

An adult snook is an apex predator with a smorgasbord of prey species to choose from and, because of its size and speed, few enemies capable of preying on it. Our young male, now about 20 to 24 inches long, is capable of eating many of the creatures in its environment that swim or crawl. It must fear only the largest, most efficient marine predators: dolphins, barracudas, and sharks. And, of course, it must avoid the deadliest predator of all: humans.

*Mangrove estuaries are fertile nurseries for juvenile snook, such as this feisty foot-long fish.* TERRY GIBSON

Although humans are arguably the most dangerous snook predators, dolphins may be the most efficient. Many of us have seen big dolphins leisurely cruising the shoreline in summer, during the peak of snook spawning activity. In an instant, these amazing cetaceans can transform from deceptively slow and playful creatures into full-speed-ahead eating machines. One July morning I watched a dolphin use its tail to smack a snook on a high arc into the air, then rocket forward like a Jet Ski for 20 feet and catch the fish in its mouth. In my observations, dolphins seem to confine their feeding to schoolie-size fish, 20 to 25 inches. I have never seen a dolphin catch and eat a really large snook.

Finally, in the second spring after its birth, our snook begins to feel the powerful pull of the spawning urge. When the northern cool fronts fade away into memory and inshore waters warm into the mid-70s, the snook joins up with others of its year class, heading out of the estuary to the beaches and passes where they were born. Studies have shown that snook, like Atlantic salmon, return to the same spawning areas year after year. Spawning begins in earnest when the water temperature reaches 80 degrees. Activity seems to vary with the phases of the moon. "It looks like there's more happening in the dark phases of the moon, like third quarter, new moon, and first quarter," Taylor says.

Cruising singly or in a school numbering from a handful to half a hundred or more, our snook seeks out one of the larger females, following and waiting, waiting nearby until the release of her eggs triggers the ejection of his sperm. It is the completion of the cycle of procreation that is as old as time. Taylor says that females spawn as often as every two days, but it is unlikely that this frequency lasts for the entire six-month season. Still, it is evident that sheer numbers of eggs and larvae—as many as 3.75 million in just one week—is an important survival mechanism. Against tough odds, the species will survive for at least another generation.

According to Taylor, accurate estimates of survival rates from egg to adult are very difficult to determine because of the daunting complications of designing a reliable scientific study. The variables are seemingly limitless and uncontrollable. "That's the holy grail of any fish's biology," he says. But one thing is clear. To get to the point where it could reproduce, our snook had to overcome many significant threats to its existence. Professor Ernst Peebles, a researcher at the University of South Florida in St. Petersburg, estimates that the mortality rate for snook and other broadcast spawners is greater than 99 percent in the first month.

To tilt the odds more in favor of species survival, snook and a number of other fish (e.g., striped bass) have evolved a reproductive adaptation that seems straight out of science fiction or a joke from *La Cage aux Folles:* they change sex. Beginning around the third year of their lives, most male snook become females. This phenomenon is called protandric hermaphroditism. This means that our snook, after spawning as a male for one season, will likely become a female at about 25 inches long (some males make the change as much as seven years later). The transformation generally takes about three months and occurs after the spawning season has ended.

As it continues to grow over the following years, our (now female) snook's increased body mass allows it to produce a greater number of eggs, further enhancing the chances of maintaining a viable population. In a sense, the sex-change tactic is a biological insurance policy.

Unfortunately, especially when human predation and habitat destruction are major factors, biology is not always enough to ensure a species' continued existence. This fact is sadly borne out by the disappearance of such creatures as the passenger pigeon and the dodo, and the decimation of countless other animal populations worldwide.

Snook have been around for a long time. Fossil records of the family Centropomidae, to which they belong, go back fifty million years, to the Eocene epoch. The genus *Centropomus* is more than three million years old, and snook as we know them—the species *undecimalis*—are at least one to two million years old. But their ability to survive for eons that included wrenching climatic changes (glaciation and melting), catastrophic astronomical events (asteroid strikes), and tectonic upheavals was no help against human greed and heedlessness.

Were it not for a handful of angry fishermen and courageous fish-and-wildlife officials, the snook might now be extinct or a remnant species in the United States. Until the mid-twentieth century, commercial fishing took a terrible toll in Florida. The same mind-set—thoughtless overharvest—that nearly led to the extirpation of plume-bearing birds in south Florida also pushed snook to the brink. It was not until 1957, in the wake of a dire population assessment and predictions of impending disaster, that the state designated snook a gamefish and halted all commercial fishing for them.

How precarious was the snook's status? In the 1960s, novelist and naturalist Peter Matthiessen published a short story titled "On the River Styx," about a fisherman in pursuit of the extremely rare snook, whose scarcity gave them near-mythical status. Fortunately, ongoing scientific studies, the development of sound management plans and regulations, and better enforcement efforts over nearly five decades have brought this magnificent gamefish back from the brink of extinction.

These days, Florida is arguably the world's greatest snook fishing destination. The nearly half-century-long prohibition on commercial snook fishing, combined with strict size and harvest limits and closed seasons during the summer spawn and the coldest winter months, has ensured that this superb gamefish will be around for future generations. Indeed, for many of us, *these* are the good old days. Population estimates put snook numbers at 1.38 million on Florida's Gulf coast and 362,000 on the Atlantic. Another important factor in the health of the snook population is the state's 1995 constitutionally mandated ban on inshore commercial gill nets. Snook were often among the by-kill of netters targeting other species, such as mullet.

A map depicting the distribution of snook populations would clearly show that they are a tropical and subtropical species of the western Atlantic. In the United States, snook's main range is central and southern Florida, although there is also a small population in south Texas. Some years, snook have been caught in significant numbers into northern Florida, and isolated fish have been found as far north as New York. Outside the United States, they are also found in Mexico, Central and South America, and some Caribbean islands.

Compared with a number of other marine gamefish, snook are homebodies. A good contrast is striped bass, another powerful, piscivorous, highly popular gamefish. Stripers are anadromous and take part in seasonal migrations that routinely cover hundreds of miles. Snook, on the other hand, are catadromous, rarely leaving their home estuaries.

Taylor, who conducted a tagging study of 35,000 snook in Tampa Bay from 1991 to 1997, found that "not a single fish left the bay." Another study in the Naples area found that 85 percent of the tagged fish were recovered within 15 miles of the tagging site. East coast Florida snook have a bit more wanderlust but are not truly migratory.

In a sense, then, snook's "lifestyle" makes them more dependable quarry than many other ocean species. An angler who hooks a snook in Tampa Bay in July also has a good chance of landing one in January. Contrast this with striper fishing in the Northeast, which, in seasonal terms, is a boom-or-bust fishery. On Cape Cod, for example, stripers may be found blitzing bait by the tens of thousands from June to October. But in January, an angler has about as much chance of finding a unicorn as a striped bass in Cape Cod Bay.

If our snook is fortunate and wary it may live another two decades, continuing to grow into a trophy fish, possibly upward of 50 pounds. The current fly-rod record is a magnificent 30-pound, 4-ounce fish caught in the Ten Thousand Islands area of the Everglades near Chokoloskee, Florida, in 1993. The all-tackle world record, 53 pounds 10 ounces, was caught in Costa Rica.

# CHAPTER 3

# A Fish for All Seasons

The sun had sunk below the mangrove shoreline and, with the temperature dropping into the 50s, it was a cool winter evening in southwest Florida. Three of us were wading the back side of Sanibel Island, casting over the grass flats on an incoming tide. As on recent evenings, our luck had been good. We had landed close to a dozen spotted seatrout and one sheepshead. And, with the light fading, the action was picking up.

I made another cast, stripped, felt the hit, and set the hook, primed for the telltale head-thrashing tugs of another seatrout. But as soon as the rod bowed over, the fish took off, instantaneously ramping up the reel's rpm to the fly fisher's favorite tune—the high-pitched *zzzzzzzzzz* that is part kazoo and part angry hornet. Within a few seconds the backing was shrinking from the spool and I reached over to tighten down on the drag. But it made little difference. The fish continued to race eastward down the shoreline. I began to follow and, raising the rod tip higher, palmed the reel to increase the pressure. Splashing through the shallows, I gained no line, but at least it was going out more slowly.

"What is it?" my pal Jim Baldwin asked as I splashed past. "Don't know," I shouted. Glancing down, I could see the black spool showing through the backing, and I palmed the reel harder, finally stopping it. Quickly I cranked in 20 feet of line, moving at flank speed toward the fish. It made another lunge, this time circling back toward shore and the mangroves, and I gained another 30 feet. Now the fight was in my favor. Another five minutes and, in the gathering dusk, I could finally see the fish: a snook longer than my arm.

"A snook?" Jim said. "The water's too cold."

My other angling partner, Dick White, waded over as I was reviving the fish. "Didn't jump at all?" he asked.

"Nope, that's why I couldn't tell."

"Huh," he said, shaking his head.

The combination of cold water and good snook fishing is about as common as a lunar eclipse. It was another lesson for three hard-core snook fly-fishing addicts: no matter how long you fish for them, they can always surprise you. It is one of the traits that make these quicksilver lightning bolts such superb gamefish.

As the previous chapter explained, understanding their life history and biology is an important factor in successful snook fishing. As with any species, snook follow broadly predictable patterns that are largely deter-

*A trophy snook may be the reward for wading a grass flat on a cool winter evening.* JIM BALDWIN

mined by their genetics, biology, and morphology. One of the most salient points in understanding snook is that these aerialist bruisers are tropical and subtropical fish; Florida is the far northern range of their habitat (though scattered catches have been reported as far north as the Carolinas and even New York). They are heat-seeking piscine torpedoes, and it is virtually impossible for the water to be too warm for them. The flip side is that they are extremely susceptible to cold water and will do anything to avoid it. Of course, cold is a relative term in Florida and the Tropics. It is not Minnesota cold, or even South Carolina cold. But it can still sometimes be too cold for snook. They become lethargic and semidormant when the water temperature falls into the low 60s, and if it drops below the mid-50s, they begin to die.

When asked the best time of year to fish for snook, my answer echoes the name of the Indian princess on *Howdy Doody*, the 1950s children's television show: Summerfall Winterspring. This means that, with the exception of rare and temporary weather aberrations, they can be caught throughout the year. They are truly a fish for all seasons. However, it is important for anglers to change areas and strategies to suit snook's seasonal patterns, which vary dramatically. When planning trips and tactics, it is paramount to understand and differentiate between the two major and sharply distinct snook fishing periods: summer and winter.

## SUMMER

"The best time of year for snook is when you sweat," a friend is fond of saying. And it is true. The summer months, with their oppressive heat and humidity, offer the most spectacular and productive kind of snook fishing for fly rodders: sight fishing along ocean beaches. In clear, shallow water, with hundreds (sometimes thousands) of hungry, cruising fish, it is the stuff of fly fishers' dreams.

Beginning usually in early to mid-May, snook migrate in large numbers out of the rivers and sheltered estuaries where they have spent the cool months. Following one of the most powerful pulls in nature—the urge to spawn—they move into passes and nearshore waters along oceanfront shorelines, where they remain in large numbers into late October.

In normal years, the hottest months—June, July, and August—are far and away the best months for beach fly fishing. This is because snook thrive in water temperatures from the mid-80s to the low 90s. Under the blazing subtropical sun, they cruise the beaches in search of spawning

*Surf, sun, and snook make for a perfect summer day on the beach.*

partners and, especially early and late in the spawning cycle, feed vora-
ciously.

Huge numbers of fish and the enlightened regulations (in Florida)
prohibiting the killing of spawning snook from May through August create
a summer catch-and-release nirvana for fly fishers. Those spin and bait
fishers who pursue them only for fillets stay home or go golfing, leaving
the beaches virtually deserted.

Most fly fishers understand that fishing is really hunting with a rod
and line. And the purest, most exciting form is sight fishing. This electrifying yet surprisingly neglected aspect of the sport begins after the passing of the spring blows. When the ocean (or Gulf) water calms and clears
over the sandbars, and inshore water temperatures climb into the mid-70s
and beyond, snook begin prowling the shallows singly, in pairs, in small
pods, and in schools of thirty or more, driven by the urge to reproduce
and smashing swarms of baitfish to provide the energy for their most
important life task.

If conditions are right—clear water and light wind—beach fishing for
snook is one of saltwater fly fishing's greatest thrills; it's just as exciting as
bonefishing, with the added kick that snook not only make long runs but
also jump. A neighbor of mine on Sanibel Island makes no bones about it:

"It's as much fun as anything I've had at Grand Cayman or Key West," Paul Ravenna says. He recalls "fantastic" days when "I saw thousands of fish coming up the beach." Anglers accustomed to working hard for one or two snook in mangrove pockets or grass-flat potholes are astounded at the abundance. "Where are all these fish coming from?" a German friend exclaimed one June afternoon after his arms got tired from catching linesiders.

This is not to say that it is always easy to catch beach snook. When the water is glassy calm and clear, they can be so spooky that they rocket away at the movement of the line against the sky. At such times, it is easy to get frustrated watching so many fish pass by. But on the best days, when water visibility is good and a light breeze riffles the surface, the action can be wild. These fish are not light-shy and will hit all day long, though they may turn on or off with the phase of the tide. Fishing at slack tide, especially slack low, is usually a waste of time.

When the fish are coming fast, this is a run-and-gun pursuit that calls for good timing, minimal false casting, and fast, accurate casts. Under these conditions, it is easy to catch snook fever. Even the most cosmopolitan fly fishers, people who have fished all over the world, can become infected the first time they spot a fast-moving pod of linesiders cruising toward them only a few feet from shore. I have seen first-rate, experienced anglers get their feet tangled in their lines, slap down a hard cast right over a school, crack the backcast like a whip, or drop a tangled bird's nest a few feet in front of them. And I have done these things myself. At such times, it is possible to expand one's vocabulary of expletives.

This kind of fishing can change as fast as the weather. If an onshore wind blows up and roils the water, the sight fishing is soon over, and it is time to either quit or fall back on the cast-and-hope technique. I have caught a good number of snook blind casting along beaches, but once you have sight fished them—and taken note of the amount of empty water between fish—it is hard to get enthused about tossing a fly into the opaque depths. If the water becomes roiled and discolored, it is a good time to head for areas of structure: blowdowns, driftwood jumbles, breakwaters, and areas of hard bottom can all be productive.

Because of the heavier Atlantic surf, the Gulf coast of Florida generally provides better beach sight fishing. The premier area is southwest Florida's barrier islands, from Cayo Costa to Marco Island. All can have good numbers of fish, but the best overall conditions—shallow water and gently sloping beaches, no high-rises or mobs of swimmers—are on Sanibel Island.

Beach snook are not choosy about the time of day. They will hit mornings and evenings, in the black of night and under the high, bright midday sun. In fact, the bright daylight hours, from about 9 A.M. to 5 P.M., are best for sight fishing. Mornings and evenings, when the sun is at a lower angle to the water, it is much harder to spot the fish.

It is still possible to catch snook in summer in estuaries, creeks, and backwaters, but the numbers are much reduced from what they are in the cooler months.

## WINTER

The February morning had dawned bright and sunny after several cloudy days with daytime air temperatures around 60 degrees and nighttime lows in the 40s. The forecast—afternoon highs in the low 70s—seemed auspicious for a snook foray into the backwaters of Sanibel Island's J. N. "Ding" Darling National Wildlife Refuge with my buddy Dave Ford.

I cast to the mangrove pocket, let my Schminnow settle for a second, and began to strip the line in short, 6-inch pulls. Once, twice, three times, and out of the gnarly roots and low-hanging branches came a wake,

*A 25-inch snook is aglow in the lowering rays of a winter sun.* DAVE FORD

shooting toward the fly. I saw a silver flash, felt a tug, and set the hook. A split second later, the white-silver fish shot out of the water, shaking its head from side to side and falling back with a splash.

"Man, did you see him hit that thing?" Ford said as I battled to force the fish away from the shoreline tangle. In a couple of minutes I brought it to the boat, gripped it by the lower jaw, and held it up, shimmering gold and silver in the winter sun. Quickly I removed the fly from the corner of its mouth with a slight twist of the hook and watched the fish shoot down and away into the tannic-stained water. Suddenly a cool, windy February day that had shown little promise was transformed. A single snook can do that.

For the next two hours, Ford and I would work our way west-southwest along the long, sheltered north shore of the mangrove bay. Using the relative stealth of a trolling motor and taking turns casting, we would boat three linesiders to break our winter drought. After a sharp, two-week cold snap with no snook at all, it seemed as great a triumph as the summer days of limitless hookups along the beaches.

Though it may seem like a contradiction, the differences between winter and summer snook fishing are both pronounced and negligible. Most evident is the contrast in angling environments. In a number of ways, winter snooking is the obverse of the summer variety. The best summer snook fishing takes place in clear water and along wide-open sandy beaches with few or no obstructions; the winter version is played out mainly in the dark, tannic-stained waters of sheltered estuaries along shorelines thick with vegetation and other natural structure.

The general parameters of winter snooking are based on snook's love of warm water. Thus, when the days get shorter, they migrate far up into rivers, canals, creeks, and harbors in search of havens from the falling temperatures (the low 70s and below) in more exposed waters. During the coolest months, they may be found far from the ocean in remote backwaters and far up freshwater streams, as well as around man-made shelters and structures such as docks, marinas, resorts, and especially power plant outflows.

The most common and productive kind of winter snook fishing—and the one depicted on all the fly-fishing television shows—is prospecting mangrove estuaries. This includes tidal and freshwater creeks, drainage ditches, and canals. Perhaps the most celebrated locale for mangrove estuary snook fishing is the Everglades National Park–Ten Thousand Islands region. The Pine Island Sound–Charlotte Harbor system is also a top destination on Florida's west coast, as is the Indian River estuary on the east coast.

One type of snook fishing that takes place year-round but can be especially hot on the coolest winter nights is fishing under dock lights. Anyone who has tried it knows what a rush this slam-bang activity—a combination of sight fishing and casting to likely lies—can be. Other top environments for winter snook are oyster bars, grass flats, and canals. When fishing around oyster bars, look for deep pockets close in to the shell reefs.

## SPRING AND FALL

Spring and fall can be considered shoulder seasons, in that they represent transition phases in snook's yearly cycle. During both periods, the fish are on the move: out of the estuaries to the beaches in the spring, and from the ocean to their backwater sanctuaries in the fall. During these seasons, snook can generally be found in good numbers in the full range of environments they inhabit.

One of the keys to deducing where the best fishing is in both spring and fall is keeping an eye on week-to-week weather trends. A string of unseasonably warm or cool days can speed up or slow down the fish's feeding and migratory patterns. The most important factor in the seasonal equation, however, is water temperature. Anglers should start haunting the ocean shore when it reaches the mid-70s in the spring. On the flip side of the calendar, the first cool fronts of fall can trigger awesome—but generally short-lived—feeding blitzes along the beaches, as snook in post-spawning mode gorge on huge schools of migrating baitfish. This phenomenon usually occurs from October to early November. When the water dips below 65 degrees, it is usually time to give up on beach fishing until the vernal equinox rolls around again.

# CHAPTER 4

# *What They Eat*

Neonatal larval snook survive initially on nutrition from their egg sacs but are soon eating microscopic animal and plant organisms —zooplankton and phytoplankton. As they grow, they expand their diets to include both the larvae and the eggs of copepods. These tiny creatures are among the most important organisms in the marine food chain and, except for microscopic life-forms, among the most numerous. They resemble tiny crabs, shrimp, or bugs. Larval snook also feed on the larval and egg stages of other marine animals, algae, and other plant matter.

In the juvenile stage—generally beginning at slightly less than 1 inch —snook begin to make the transformation to their adult eating pattern, which is primarily piscivorous (fish eating). Although the juvenile phase begins with a diet of predominantly adult copepods and insects, the fry of other fish soon become important food sources as the snook gain length and weight. As the Florida Marine Research Institute's Ron Taylor notes, however, the sizes at which these developmental changes take place can vary. One study showed that at slightly more than half an inch, juvenile snook consume about 90 percent copepods and other microinvertebrates and 10 percent fish. But the conversion comes quickly. By the time they reach 1 inch, the ratio is, in effect, inverted. High on the list of piscine prey are anchovies, glass minnows, pinfish, mosquito fish, grass shrimp, and killifish.

Although the facts about the feeding habits of larval and juvenile snook are interesting as general information, what really interests fly fishers, of course, is what the big boys and girls eat. The final transition—to adulthood and sexual maturity—takes place when a snook reaches a length of about 14 to 19 inches.

Adult snook are rapacious, undiscriminating feeders, consuming a mixed diet. In order of importance, this includes baitfish, crustaceans, and a few mollusks. Snook can generally be described as omnivorous carnivores. Only rarely do they eat algae and aquatic vegetation.

· Common prey species include ladyfish, mullet, shrimp, small calico crabs, sand fleas (aka sand crabs), worms, glass minnows, shad, pilchards, needlefish, seatrout, greenbacks, pinfish, threadfin herring, grunts, pigfish, sailfin mollies, menhaden, and mojarras. Less common are small blue crabs, pass crabs, and mangrove crabs. But like other piscine apex predators (e.g., largemouth bass in fresh water), snook will eat anything that does not try to eat them first and fits in their mouths. This reputedly includes baby alligators in freshwater areas, baby sea turtles along the beaches, and lizards and snakes that drop from the mangroves, although some of these tales may be apocryphal.

For fly fishers, the most important lesson to learn from snook feeding patterns is this: stick to flies that imitate the most common prey species. In other words, although it would no doubt be fun to tie a sea turtle or

*Pinfish.*

*Greenback.*

*Grass shrimp.*

*Blue crab.*

alligator imitation, it would probably not catch many fish. Nine times out of ten, snook prefer to eat baitfish. Most of the baitfish that snook eat are silvery white, green and white, or gold and white, so pick flies that are similar in color. If there are large numbers of one kind of baitfish in a particular area, it is a good idea to try to "match the hatch." Size is also an important factor. If snook are feeding on 2-inch whitebait, it makes little sense to throw a 4-inch Deceiver at them.

Looking at it anthropomorphically, snook are classy eaters, taking their meals fresh and on the go. Only rarely are they caught on dead bait. And unlike redfish and bonefish, they almost never root around in the mud and the sand to expose bottom-digging critters. It follows that fly fishers should work their flies anywhere from high to low in the water column, but not on the bottom. In general, it is better to fish too shallow than too deep. This is because of snook's anatomical structure (upward-looking eyes) and their behavior (an overwhelming preference to attack from below or from the same depth).

Snook are high-powered attack feeders, not foragers or scavengers. Seeing their prey is much more important than smelling it. And they are very efficient predators. Like wolves and lions, they specialize in attack and ambush styles of hunting. Another trait they have in common with these land predators is that they key in on the weak and wounded among their prey.

In open water, snook are active hunters, cruising and searching far and wide until they find baitfish pods to attack. But they are also frugal with their energy. They can be spotted swimming in the middle of huge schools of bait, moving with the mass, waiting and watching to spot a vulnerable individual before rushing in for the kill. Just as caribou do with wolves and zebras with lions, baitfish tolerate snook within a certain proximity. In clear water, anglers should look for white holes in the middle of large bait swarms to find the snook.

Contrary to what some people think, fly anglers can have great success, no matter how much live prey is in the water. The right tactics are the secret to catching fish. Cast to the forward edge of the open spot, and strip the fly slowly away from the snook or diagonally across its swimming lane, twitching and pausing it. These are the trigger signals that imitate a wounded baitfish, and often the snook will shoot through the masses of healthy live fish to grab the imitation.

In the mangroves, snook typically follow an ambush feeding strategy, lurking in secluded pockets, among roots, and under overhanging branches and then darting out to grab careless baitfish that stray too near. Just like freshwater trout, they prefer to grab food that comes to them—expending as little energy as possible—so be sure to get the fly as close as you can to the structure and vegetation, preferably within a foot or less. There is a snook anglers' saying that if you are not occasionally getting your fly hung up in the mangroves, you are not casting tight enough.

# CHAPTER 5

# *Tactics and Equipment*

Many spin fishers and bait casters who target snook are intrigued by the idea of fly fishing. Unfortunately, they are sometimes intimidated, and thus hesitant to try it, because of three major misconceptions:

1. Fly fishing means handicapping yourself.
2. Techniques are complicated and difficult to learn.
3. Equipment is esoteric, expensive, innumerable, and arcane.

All these statements are far off the mark. In most situations, fly fishing is at least as effective as any other method of catching snook. In fact, knowledgeable fly fishers who adapt their gear and tactics for different locations and conditions can often outfish bait fishers and plug casters.

A classic example is my favorite kind of snook fishing: sight casting along beaches during the summer spawning season. On clear-water days with little wind, beach fish can be incredibly spooky. Any advantage is a plus, and this is where flies truly come into their own. The basic physics and mechanics of spin fishing and bait casting require weighted baits, either artificial or natural. This means they always land with a splash, a splat, or a plop, and in clear water, that means good-bye snook.

One day, about a mile from my house on Sanibel Island, I walked down the beach past a spin fisherman standing in the water up to his thighs and casting a lead-head white curly-tail jig while his wife watched from a beach chair. The snook were cruising the shoreline in large numbers, as they do only during the summer spawn, and they were ripe for the catching. But every time he cast to a single, a pair, or a school, the fish spooked.

I walked 50 yards past him and, in half an hour, casting a No. 2 Schminnow, landed nine fish, lost half a dozen others, and had at least ten follows. Because I had an appointment in town, I had to leave, even though the fish were still cruising and hitting. When I walked back past the couple, the wife spoke up. "You must have been in a perfect spot down there," she said. The husband, still fishless, gave her a withering glance. As gently as I could, I explained that I was casting to some of the same fish that had swum past them.

One fault with his tactics was that he was standing in the fish's cruising lane instead of on the shore. Some of them were passing behind him, between where he stood and the sloping beach. But the key reason for my success and his lack of it was that my Schminnow was landing as softly as a feather in the snook's feeding zone—2 or 3 feet in front of the fish— whereas his jig hit with a clearly audible *plup,* causing a tiny geyser and

*In clear water, summer snook often cruise within a few feet of shore.*

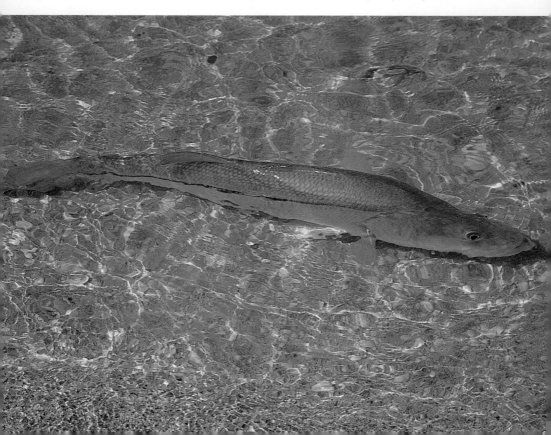

a ring of wavelets. As soon as the lure landed, the snook headed for Cuba. The same "soft landing" advantage applies when fly fishing on shallow grass flats and under dock lights when the fish are near the surface.

The basic techniques of fly fishing for snook are no more difficult to learn than any other kind of fishing. Most important is the cast. In my experience, even rank beginners can master the basic skill required—the ability to throw 30 to 40 feet of line and leader—after an hour or less of instruction. The rest, as they say, takes a lifetime.

Becoming a good caster—a combination of accuracy and distance— increases one's chance of success with snook. This comes with practice and time on the water. But in my experience, the difference in numbers of fish caught by good casters and exceptional casters is minimal. Although double hauling provides the distinct advantage of added distance, it is not a prerequisite. It is not necessary to cast half a mile like the celebrity anglers on television. Likewise, tournament-level casting skills, such as being able to cast the whole fly line and make trick casts, while great for wowing the crowds at industry expos, do not have a close correlation with snook angling success.

After the cast, the retrieve is the next most important factor in technique. There are three basic retrieves, depending on the type of fly: streamer, weighted streamer, spoon fly, slider, gurgler, or popper. For the most popular streamers, such as Deceivers, Clousers, Schminnows, Cockroaches, Snapping Shrimp, etc., the standard streamer retrieve of strip-pause-strip-pause is highly effective. Some of the other categories of flies have their own ideal retrieves, which are generally variations on the standard.

Just as in other types of fly fishing, the list of essential equipment for snook is straightforward and short: rod, reel, fly line, backing, leader, and flies. Additional, optional items, such as stripping basket, vest or fanny pack, and wading boots, are useful in different situations but not essential. A rundown of the basic equipment is presented next, followed by tips for landing snook. Flies are covered in chapter 6.

## RODS

As in all fly fishing, the most important piece of equipment is the rod. The best all-around design for snook is a 7- or 8-weight fast-action model that measures $8\frac{1}{2}$ to 9 feet long. Rods with these specifications are available from all the major manufacturers. The stiffness of a fast-action model allows for more effective casting (especially tighter loops) under windy conditions and provides superior fish-fighting power over slower, softer rods.

Power and stiffness combined with light weight are the keys to deriving the most pleasure from the sport, and there is no question that this means high-modulus graphite composite construction. Some of the newer rods with added elements, such as titanium or boron, provide even better strength-to-weight ratios than graphite alone. The few fiberglass rods still on the market—heavy, soft, and frustratingly sluggish—are technological anachronisms and learning handicaps. Bamboo, although an intriguing part of our fly-fishing heritage, should be avoided. The slow action, delicate presentation, and aesthetic elegance of bamboo that endear it to many traditional trout fishers have no place in saltwater angling. Despite their elegance, comfort, and quality of design, using bamboo rods for snook fishing would be like running a track event in Armani loafers.

Anglers who fish mainly mangrove shorelines sometimes favor 9- or even 10-weight rods, arguing that these are better for turning a fish that heads for structure, such as roots or dock pilings. But in most cases, the extra heft and backbone are unnecessary if the proper tactics are employed. (Most important is keeping the rod tip in the water and pulling at a 90-degree angle to the fish's direction to turn its head.) One big negative of a heavier rod is that the extra weight (of both the line and the rod) increases the angler's fatigue factor. This is an especially important consideration when blind casting in mangrove estuaries, when it is not unusual to make hundreds of casts during a day's outing. Most people who have suffered from the fly fisher's version of tennis elbow (the medical term is lateral epicondylitis)—an ailment that is unfortunately all too common—are eager to adopt any measures that reduce the chance of a recurrence. Heavier rods and lines also put more stress on the casting shoulder and muscles.

Another major reason for choosing lighter gear is the stealth factor. Especially under sight-fishing conditions, a lighter line lands more softly, decreasing the chances of spooking fish. The sporting aspect of lighter rods is an additional plus. Not all the snook you catch will be 30 inches or more; in fact, the majority will measure 18 to 24 inches. Just as using a 7-weight would take much of the fun out of dapping for 6-inch brook trout, winching in 20-inch snook with a 10-weight outfit would be a less satisfying experience. It must be acknowledged, however, that a heavier rod and line combination generally provides greater casting distance and better control in windy conditions.

Performance is important, but for most anglers, price is also a consideration. Top-of-the-line outfits—rod, reel, and line—start at around $800. But for neophytes, it makes sense to begin more modestly. Many major manufacturers, angling supply companies, and outdoor equipment catalogs (L. L. Bean, Bass Pro Shops, Albright, Orvis, Cabela's, and others) offer good-quality entry-level outfits for around $200. Once anglers learn the basic mechanics and techniques of the sport, they will be better able to judge their own personal skills and equipment preferences and upgrade their gear accordingly.

## REELS

I admit to a deep-seated bias in favor of inexpensive reels. The old saw that a reel is merely a place to store line has more than a grain of truth to it. This is not to say that snook anglers should buy junk. The most important factor when choosing a reel is that it should be designed and manufactured for use in salt water. This means that the internal components are constructed to be more corrosive resistant than those in freshwater reels. In saltwater reels, the gears, spindles, drags, and so forth are usually made of stainless steel, brass, nylon, or other synthetic materials.

Cast or machined aluminum alloy is the material of choice for the spools and casings of many saltwater fly reels. But in recent years, composite polymer graphite reels have come into their own. They are even lighter than aluminum, again reducing the arm, joint, and shoulder strain associated with frequent and arduous fly-fishing outings.

One of the most important qualities for a snook reel is a reliable disk drag. Although snook do not have the breathtaking speed of bonefish, they can make multiple swift, powerful runs. As with other powerful saltwater gamefish—stripers, redfish, bluefish—the drag is an important tool for wearing them down so they can be landed within a time frame that enhances survivability. It is possible to use a click drag reel by palming the spool during runs (also an effective adjunct tactic any time), but a disk drag is more straightforward and dependable, especially for beginners.

Reel spool size is another factor to consider. The three basic choices are small arbor (traditional), medium arbor, and large arbor. I favor medium- and large-arbor models because the spool's greater diameter enables faster line retrieval than conventional models. The one disadvantage to large-arbor spools is that they do not hold as much line and backing. Medium-arbor spools provide a compromise; they allow more space for line storage while facilitating a somewhat faster fight and retrieve than the traditional models.

Good, standard-production saltwater fly reels start at around $50 and range up to hundreds of dollars. For custom-built reels, the sky is the limit. Choosing a reel is partly a matter of weighing the relative importance of initial expenditure versus durability. In general, the higher the cost, the longer the life expectancy of the reel. Higher-end reels are engineered to last—with proper care—for a lifetime of normal fishing.

## FLY LINES

For beginning fly fishers, the decision of which line to buy can seem especially daunting. The choices may seem endless, and the myriad specifications and intended uses baffling. Should they pick floating, intermediate sink, full sink, sinking tip, clear tip, weight forward, double taper, triangle taper, level, etc.? Fortunately, for snook anglers, the choice is easy: a weight-forward, floating line that matches the rod weight. Because snook are inshore, shallow-water fish, sinking lines are necessary only in limited situations.

The characteristics of a weight-forward line—thicker and heavier at the casting end—provide the best control for casting saltwater flies greater distances accurately. They also help overcome one of the most common saltwater fly-fishing bugaboos: wind.

Because they are thinner and lighter at both ends, double-taper lines, the choice of many freshwater trout anglers, are not well suited for snook fishing. The extra stealth provided by a finer line that lands more softly—especially advantageous for dry-fly trout fishing in small, smooth waters—is not exactly superfluous for snook (there is no such thing as too much stealth), but it is outweighed by the disadvantages of the slim taper in casting large flies under breezy conditions.

Because most snook fishing takes place in shallow water, a floating line is the best choice more than 90 percent of the time. In those few situations when it is necessary to get the fly down a bit more (e.g., potholes on flats, deeper mangrove pockets), the extra depth can usually be achieved by using a weighted fly such as a Clouser. However, experienced snookers usually carry an extra spool with an intermediate- or full-sink line for those rare occasions (pass or channel fishing) when greater depth is required.

These days, fly lines come in a mind-boggling array of colors, from comparatively drab tans and beiges to bright yellow and hot pink. The common argument is that the brilliant colors provide greater line visibility for anglers. This is a specious argument. Neither I nor anyone I know has ever had trouble spotting his or her line on the water. Neutral colors are by far the best for snook fishing: light blue, tan, beige, off-white. Despite the advertising claims, brilliant colored lines are more effective at catching fishermen than fish. And I am convinced that in some conditions—such as sight fishing in clear water—their heightened visibility can spook the fish both in the air (during false casts) and in the water. Brightly colored lines also necessitate longer leaders, making casting more difficult at close distances. Several companies offer clear sinking lines, and it is a shame that there is currently no clear floating line on the market.

## BACKING

Backing is the line loaded onto the reel spool first, to which the fly line is tied. Because fly lines are short—generally no more than 110 feet—backing enables anglers to successfully fight and land big fish that run great distances.

A good saltwater fly caster can cast 70 or 80 feet of fly line. Without backing, even a medium-size snook would soon reach the end of the line, and that would often be the end of the fight, because the leader tippet would break under the full, direct power of the fish's pull. Many people, however, overload their reels with more backing than necessary. In my experience, 50 yards of line is enough for all but the largest snook. One hundred yards is adequate for most of these, and 125 yards provides an extra margin for extenuating circumstances, such as heavy current.

Braided Dacron line is the best backing choice. Again, I prefer a common, dull color such as white or beige. Some brightly colored braided lines, such as chartreuse or blaze orange, contain dyes that can discolor the fly line. Dacron provides a good test strength-to-diameter ratio. An 18- to 20-pound-test line is heavy enough for excellent fish-fighting performance and thin enough to permit a full-length load while allowing plenty of spool space for the fly line. A reel that is overfilled, with the fly line bumping the struts, is an aggravation and a hindrance.

**LEADERS**

Snook leaders should be good-quality tapered monofilament or fluorocarbon. They should be a minimum of $7^1/_2$ feet long with at least 10-pound tippet strength. The exact specifications vary with the type of snook fishing. In clear water, the leader should be 9 feet or more, and the tippet strength should be on the light side for greater stealth. In dark water and around structure, shorter leaders and higher tippet strength—up to 30 pounds—are called for.

Finished leaders can be purchased in extrusion tapers—one continuous length of material that tapers from the butt to the tippet—or knotted tapers—materials of different strengths tied together in a series, from heaviest to lightest. Many anglers prefer to tie their own leaders, both to save money and to ensure that the specifications are exactly what they want.

Snook leaders can also be used for spotted seatrout, redfish, jack crevalle, bonefish, and many other subtropical and tropical saltwater species. But for snook, there is one extra element that is indispensable: a bite tippet. Unlike the piranha-like choppers of bluefish, Spanish mackerel, and other species, snook's tiny, sandpaper teeth are deceptively benign, but they are so abrasive that they can quickly cut through light- or medium-weight tippet material. Snook also have razor-sharp gill plates that can slice through a light tippet in the blink of an eye when they jump or make a sudden sharp turn.

When I first started snook fishing, I foolishly ignored the counsel of a longtime snook fisherman to make sure to tie a short length of heavier line to the end of the leader. I was using a tapered leader with a 12-pound tippet, and it seemed more than adequate to fight and land the fish I had observed cruising the beach near my house. But my angling hubris was quickly dispelled. The first fish I cast to and hooked made a short run, jumped, and popped the tippet. So did the second and the third. Finally, I had to admit that my acquaintance's advice was valid. I added a 1-foot section of 30-pound-test monofilament and began landing fish.

Tests have demonstrated that fluorocarbon is less visible than monofilament under water, but, having used both kinds of leaders extensively, I am not convinced that this makes a difference in the number of snook caught. And the price difference—fluorocarbon costs at least four times as much as monofilament—is significant. However, fluorocarbon's excellent abrasion resistance makes it the ideal material for bite tippets. My leader

*Large schools of cruising fish cause many a case of snook fever.*

rig of choice is a tapered monofilament leader with a tippet strength of 16 pounds and a 1-foot piece of 25-pound-test fluorocarbon bite tippet on the end. I prefer to attach the bite tippet with a blood knot (less visibility), but some anglers use a loop-to-loop connection to make it easier to change tippets.

One cautionary note: Because fluorocarbon is so much harder than monofilament, knotted fluorocarbon is more difficult to compress. This means that fluorocarbon knots do not tighten down as easily as standard monofilament does. It is important to lubricate fluorocarbon knots well (with saliva) when tying them and to make doubly sure that they are pulled snug. More times than I care to admit (usually in the excitement of pursuing big schools of moving snook on the beach), I have tied on a fly with a hasty loop knot and lost both fish and fly when the knot pulled loose. Another important consideration is checking the end of the bite tippet after every hookup. If it is frayed even a little bit, clip it back and retie the fly. It will save you lost fish.

## KNOTS

When it comes to knots for snook fishing, I follow that good old military acronym KISS—keep it simple, stupid. Only four basic knots are required. In order of importance, they are the loop knot, the improved clinch knot, the blood knot, and the nail knot.

### Loop Knot

The loop knot is ideal for attaching the fly to the bite tippet. The most important reason for using a loop knot is to allow the fly to swing and dance freely with a natural baitfish action when it is stripped. Some anglers also like to tie a loop knot on the end of a tapered leader and attach the bite tippet with a loop-to-loop connection. This makes it a simple matter to change the bite tippet when it becomes too short or frayed. The leader can be attached to the fly line with a loop-to-loop connection as well.

There are several good loop knots that are simple to tie and relatively slip-free. Choose the one that is easiest for you to remember. Be sure to tie small loops so that they are less visible to the fish.

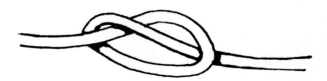

1. Tie a loose overhand knot in the leader tippet a couple of inches from the end.

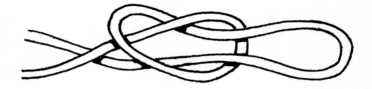

2. Insert the end of the tippet back through the overhand knot to form a small loop below the overhand knot.

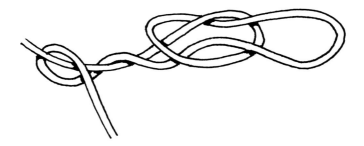

3. Wrap the end of the tippet toward you, making two turns around the leader above the overhand knot.

4. Insert the end back through the overhand knot once more.

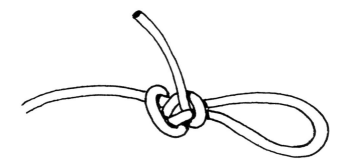

5. Lubricate with saliva and pull tight. Clip the tippet end close to the knot.

**Improved Clinch Knot**

The improved clinch knot, the old standby for dry-fly trout fishing with fine tippets, should be used sparingly by snook anglers. Because of its stiffness, a standard 25- or 30-pound-test fluorocarbon snook bite tippet severely restricts the action of a typical No. 2 snook streamer if it is tied to the fly with a clinch knot. Once in a great while I use a clinch knot to tie on a popping fly.

1. Insert the leader tippet through the eye of the hook to form a loop. Wrap the leader end five times around the line away from the hook eye. Insert the leader end back through the initial loop.

2. Insert the leader end through the second loop. Lubricate with saliva and carefully pull tight.

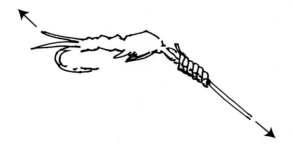

## Blood Knot

The blood knot is used for tying knotted tapered leaders. It can also be used to attach the bite tippet to the tapered leader.

1. Hold two lines or sections of leader side by side, with the ends pointing in opposite directions and one line laid across the other. The lines should overlap each other by about three inches.

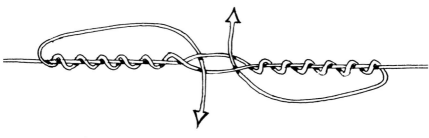

2. Wrap the ends of the lines in opposite directions away from the point of initial overlap. Insert the line ends back through the center loop in opposite directions.

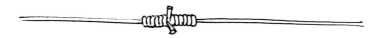

3. Lubricate with saliva and carefully pull tight. Clip the line ends close to the knot.

## Nail Knot

The nail knot is most useful for attaching the leader to the fly line if there is no loop on the end of the fly line.

All these knots should be lubricated with saliva during tying. Otherwise, they may weaken from overheating and stress when they are pulled tight.

1. Lay the leader butt, fly line end, and nail (or toothpick, knitting needle, hollow tube, etc.) side by side, with the ends of the leader butt and the fly line pointing in opposite directions. The ends should overlap by several inches.

2. Wrap the leader butt around the fly line and nail in the direction toward the end of the fly line.

3. Make at least six turns of the leader butt end around the fly line and the nail.

4. Pass the end of the leader butt back through the wraps, running it between the fly line and the nail (or through the tube).

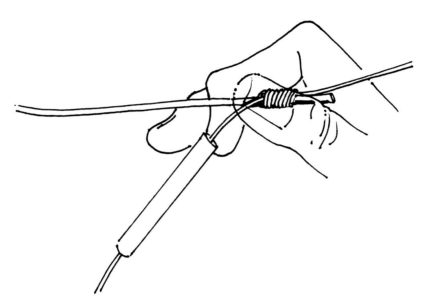

5. Slowly slide out the nail (or tube) while pulling on the long end of the leader so the wraps tighten evenly around the fly line.

6. Lubricate the knot with saliva and slowly pull it tight. Clip the ends of the leader butt and fly line close to the knot.

*A cheap and functional stripping basket constructed from a department store shopping basket.*

## STRIPPING BASKETS

Stripping baskets are rarely necessary in fresh water (steelhead and salmon fishing are two exceptions). But because of the longer casts and run-and-gun techniques required, they are an important item of gear for many kinds of saltwater fly fishing. For snook fishing, they serve two main purposes: storing line so it can be "shot" out quickly with one or two false casts, and keeping the line out from underfoot.

Stripping baskets are almost indispensable for casting from shore or the shallows, where sand, rocks, shells, driftwood, seaweed, and other materials can dirty, damage, or foul the line, and even small waves can tangle the line around an angler's legs. Stripping baskets are also very practical for use in boats, especially boats that are not specifically designed for fly fishing. Such craft often contain exposed hardware that can snare a fly line. Even when fishing from clean-hulled flats boats, many anglers use stripping baskets. These devices store the line neatly between casts and preclude the aggravation of stepping on it in the excitement of the hunt.

There are two main styles of stripping basket: the rigid plastic box style and the mesh basket style. Both have their advantages and adherents. The most basic rigid plastic version is the so-called New Jersey style: a square, plastic dishpan with holes drilled in two sides and strapped around the waist with a bungee cord. This style is not only practical but, at less than $10, also a bargain. Equipment suppliers offer more expensive, more elaborate variations on the same theme. Instead of bungee cords, most are equipped with adjustable plastic or nylon belts and snap buckles that make them easy to put on and take off. Many also have egg-carton-style inserts or built-in conical projections designed to reduce line tangles. Some

*The New Jersey–style stripping basket is adapted from a plastic dishpan.*

Florida Sportsman *editor Jeff Weakley swears by Charlie's Total Control stripping basket, a nylon mesh design stretched over a foldable wire frame.*

have cutouts on the sides that enable a rod to be laid across the basket without rolling off. Others are curved on the side that fits against the waist.

One advantage of rigid-style baskets is also a disadvantage: because they are closed boxes, they tend to keep water out during wading, but if water does get in, it cannot drain out (although a few models have drain holes).

Mesh baskets, in contrast, are designed to drain water immediately. But when wading in deep water, the water flows in just as easily. A mesh basket is of little use when it is even partially submerged. An angler might as well strip the line onto the water surface with no basket. Also, many mesh baskets are irritatingly floppy, sometimes collapsing on themselves.

My favorite stripping basket is a lightweight, box-shaped, nylon mesh model sold by a small Florida company. The key to the design of Charlie's Total Control stripping basket is an internal wire frame that provides the rigidity lacking in other mesh models. Because the frame is curved, it also has the unique quality of folding in on itself to the size of a saucer, making it much easier to store and pack for travel than other stripping baskets. I have never had one collapse during use.

## VESTS AND FANNY PACKS

Because most snook fishing takes place in warm or hot weather, light-weight nylon and mesh vests are preferred. Some anglers use fanny packs, but a vest has more storage space for fly boxes and other incidental items, such as leaders, bite tippet spools, flashlight, hemostat, and clipper.

## WADING BOOTS

Boots are optional for some snook fishing, particularly along sandy shore-lines with few sharp rocks, shells, or detritus. But they are absolutely essential for grass flats, where shells, crabs, stingrays, glass, junk, and jetsum are hard to spot and can cause painful injuries.

Flats boots are designed with thick, hard soles to resist penetration by sharp objects and, in the standard height—about 9 inches—also offer moderate protection for the ankles and lower legs. I prefer boots with neoprene uppers and nylon zippers because they are easy to put on and remove; however, canvas-top, lace-up versions offer a bit more penetration protection higher up. There are now a few brands on the market with heavy-duty uppers.

Some beach snook anglers wear wading sandals, which protect the bottoms of the feet but not the ankles, lower legs, or toes. In my opinion, this makes them next to useless. Liking the feel of sand between my toes is a vestige of my Cape Cod childhood, but I have cut my feet more than a few times.

It is important to keep in mind that where there are snook there are often stingrays. The larger, free-swimming rays, which are prevalent in large schools along summer beaches, present few problems in clear water, and they avoid anglers if possible. But the small, bottom-hugging varieties are so well camouflaged that they are virtually invisible when lying motionless in the sand. Wading boots offer a good measure of protection from an excruciatingly painful (though usually not dangerous) sting that can quickly end a fishing outing.

Deck shoes or sneakers are the most practical and comfortable footwear for boat fishing, although many anglers prefer to fish barefoot from the skid-free bow platforms of flats boats.

## SUNGLASSES

Polarized sunglasses enable wearers to see through the surface glare of the water. They are important for every kind of fishing, but for snook fly anglers they are indispensable. Those who do not use them are intention-ally handicapping themselves, choosing, for all intents and purposes, to fish partially blind. Although the high-end brands provide better vision and lens quality and are more durable, perfectly serviceable wraparound-style polarized sunglasses are available for as little as $15. As the credit card ad says, don't leave home without them.

## HOOK REMOVERS

All fly fishers should carry a hemostat or small needle-nose pliers to quickly unhook their fish and release them as gently as possible. Without this kind of tool, it can be next to impossible to remove a fly that is lodged deep in a snook's throat. A hemostat is preferable because it can be easily clipped onto and removed from a vest or shirt pocket.

## SNOOK TACTICS: FIGHTING THE GOOD FIGHT

From start to finish, fighting a snook is a unique experience that requires some tactical adjustments for many fly fishers, especially freshwater anglers.

In the beginning, of course, comes the strike. Because of their fiercely predatory nature, their ability to explode with quick bursts of speed, and their ambush feeding strategies, a snook strike is almost never tentative. They may miss the fly occasionally, swirling behind it or possibly smash-ing it first in an attempt to wound the intended prey before actually eating it. Occasionally, they chase a fly for distances of up to 40 feet before attacking or turning away, but once a snook has made the decision to get its prey, there is no such thing as a gentle take. In other words, snook fish-ing has no equivalent to a brown trout's leisurely, educated inspection of the food sources floating past its visual "window," followed by a casual, sipping take.

Snook usually attack the fly from an angle, coming at it diagonally before grabbing it and turning sharply to one side or the other an instant after the strike. As a result, the most common outcome of a snook strike is also one of the best: a clean hookup in the corner of the jaw. Sometimes, however, a snook races up behind the fly to grab it, flaring its gills wide while snapping open its enormous mouth. This creates a powerful vacuum effect that can suck the hook deep down into the gullet.

Redfish devotees know that these fish can be more fastidious feeders than snook. When they take a fly from behind, they sometimes continue swimming forward while chomping the fly to determine whether it is really food. When this happens, an angler must be very quick on the trigger and set the hook with a superfast strip. Otherwise, the red will spit out the faux baitfish, shrimp, or crab faster than a tobacco chewer spewing a spent plug. In contrast, snook's innate ferocity simplifies the hookup. They almost never short-strike. And because they attack with speed and almost always grab and turn, they usually hook themselves. However, anglers should strip-strike anyway to make sure the hook penetrates the snook's tough lips and mouth cartilage.

To make a strip strike, point the rod directly at the fish and yank back on the fly line hard and fast. The strip strike is as different from the deliberative, rod-raising hook set of dry-fly trout anglers as ballet is from professional wrestling. And because of the differences in tackle strength—specifically, rods and tippets—there is no need to be tentative in snook fishing.

Once the fish is hooked, fight it hard and fast to prevent exhaustion and lactic acid buildup in its body. Both factors increase the mortality rate of fish that are caught and released. Keep a tight drag and, if necessary, palm the reel spool to put even more pressure on the fish. In wide-open areas—beach shorelines, grass flats, and the like—the standard tip-high technique works well. But be careful not to keep the tip too high, or a big snook may break your rod.

Around structure, especially in the mangroves, use the down-and-dirty technique. Keep the rod tip low (in the water is often best), and pull the line at a 90-degree angle from the direction the fish is headed. This usually turns its head and forces it out away from the structure. Apply the maximum force your tackle can handle, for these are make-or-break situations. The alternative to keeping maximum pressure on the fish is a virtually guaranteed breakoff if it gets into roots, rocks, or pilings. Again, be careful not to put too severe a bend in the rod. Even the most expensive graphite fiber will fail if overstressed. This is a major risk when fishing from a boat if a fish makes a sudden dash under the hull.

Once you have landed (or boated) a snook, if you intend to release it, you are responsible for making sure that it swims away to propagate the species and/or be caught another day. In addition to proper fighting technique, a big part of survival success for snook is gentle handling and careful revival. Small snook—less than 20 inches—can usually be whipped and brought to hand quickly enough to make revival unnecessary. Often they dart away as soon as they are unhooked.

*A snook that gets into oyster-covered mangrove roots can cut a leader in a split second.*

Special care is necessary for larger fish, however. Keep the fish in the water, if possible. If you want to take a photograph or must lift the fish out of the water to remove the fly, get it back in as quickly as possible. A good rule of thumb is not to keep it out of the water longer than you can comfortably hold your breath. The best way to hold a fish for a photo is by supporting it with one hand under the head and the other under the slim part of the body just ahead of the tail. Never lift a large snook only by its lower jaw, especially with one of the grip-type scales. Its body weight will put a terrible strain on the muscles that control the jaw, throat, and mouth, possibly tearing them and making it next to impossible for the fish to catch food. If you are intent on weighing the fish, put it in a net and grip the net's mesh with the scale. Better yet, do not weigh the fish at all. I have measured many a snook during my longtime love affair with linesiders, but I have never weighed one.

Reviving a snook calls for the same technique used with other fish: moving it back and forth slowly in the water so the gills are oxygenated. A unique twist with snook is the "sucking the thumb" revival method. If you insert your thumb into a snook's mouth up to the first knuckle, the fish generally clamps onto it, enabling you to revive it by pushing and pulling with one hand. The fish usually signals when it is sufficiently revived by spitting out your thumb and scooting away.

It is important not to be in a rush when reviving snook, especially for trophy fish that have fought a long, hard battle prior to being landed. Make sure the fish is breathing strongly and is able to maintain its equilibrium before allowing it to swim away beyond your reach.

# CHAPTER 6

# *The Best Snook Flies*

There are six major categories of snook flies: streamers, weighted streamers, spoon flies, poppers, gurglers, and sliders. One important thing to remember when selecting snook flies is that bigger is not better. Most effective snook flies are tied in sizes from 2 to 1/0. Beginning snook anglers, particularly avid striped bass fishers, are sometimes skeptical about this axiom, especially when pursuing large snook. But as a guide friend of mine likes to remind them, elephants love peanuts.

## STREAMERS
Streamers are by far the most popular and effective type of snook fly. They are the go-to patterns for anglers of all skill and experience levels. When in doubt, try a streamer first. The reason for this is as basic as snook's feeding behavior, which is 90 percent piscivorous. Snook eat other fish nearly all the time, and most streamers imitate baitfish.

The most important retrieve rule for snook streamers is to take it easy. Snook react best to a slow retrieve with short (6- to 8-inch) strips and long pauses in between. The fish often hit a streamer on the "fall," when the fly dips down an inch or two during the pause between strips. This movement simulates the action of a wounded baitfish struggling to keep from sinking to the bottom.

The leisurely snook retrieve can present a major adjustment for striped bass anglers who are pursuing snook for the first time. Many of them have conditioned themselves to strip as fast as possible—sometimes even two-handed. Also, their strips are usually too long—18 inches or more at a pull—with little or no pause in between.

A variation on the standard snook streamer retrieve is the so-called shrimp retrieve: two short, fast strips followed by a brief pause, a single fast strip, and a long pause. The pattern is then repeated.

Although a slow retrieve is the rule, it is not absolute. When sight fishing to snook that follow the fly for more than 4 or 5 feet, it is a good idea to vary the speed and rhythm of the retrieve to try to provoke a strike. Speed it up first, and if that does not do the trick, slow it down again. Continue the retrieve all the way in. I have hooked fish 6 inches from shore and right beside the hull of a boat.

The most common baitfish in the snook's diet all share one major characteristic: coloration. Pilchards, threadfin herring, menhaden, finger mullet, greenbacks, glass minnows, and other species are all predominantly white or silver-white. It follows that the best flies, the ones that catch the most snook, reflect this fact. A few of the top snook streamers are described here.

*Norm's Crystal Schminnow:* I originally created this fly for summer sight fishing along the beaches, but in more than ten years of snook fishing—usually several times a week, and sometimes several times a day for weeks—it has been the most productive pattern in all four seasons and in every type of aquatic environment where snook are found. The Schminnow is one of the simplest patterns in the sport, but it is deadly effective. The tail is white marabou, the body is pearl-white crystal chenille or estaz, and the eyes are black monofilament. The tail is clipped to the length of the shank, so the fly imitates not only a baitfish but also a shrimp or a sand flea (sand crab). Hence the name Schminnow—part shrimp, part minnow. It does not exactly match any snook prey, but it hints at many.

Though designed with snook in mind, the Schminnow has caught twenty-nine other species in both salt and fresh water. One important consideration is that it is highly effective for all the major gamefish that live in the same habitats where snook are found. Redfish, spotted seatrout, jack crevalle, ladyfish, mangrove snapper, Spanish mackerel, and baby tarpon all love it. When tied on a circle hook, it results in a dramatic jump in the number of baby tarpon hooked and landed, but a standard J hook is just as effective for snook.

The Schminnow is designed to suspend a few inches below the surface, which is generally the best zone for the upward-looking snook.

Occasionally it is bumped along a clean bottom in shallow water to imitate a sand flea, shrimp, or other crustacean. It is also highly durable: I have caught as many as nine snook on one fly.

*Lefty's Deceiver:* Lefty Kreh's legendary streamer is probably the most famous saltwater fly pattern in the world. Although it is tied in a wide array of hues, three color patterns are particularly effective for snook: green and white, yellow and white, and silver and white. In my experience, the best is silver and white, with green (chartreuse) and white a close second.

The taper, profile, eyes, and overall length make the Deceiver strictly a baitfish pattern. Like the Schminnow, if stripped conventionally, it suspends high in the water column. However, it is useless as a bottom bumper. Deceivers are sometimes tied in bright colors, such as red and orange, as attractor patterns not intended to imitate any baitfish species. In all its versions, the Deceiver catches a wide variety of fish besides snook.

*Some of the top snook streamers. From top left: Norm's Crystal Schminnow, chartreuse and white Lefty's Deceiver, dark green and white Lefty's Deceiver, Cockroach, Glass Minnow, Soluble Minnow, Everglades Special, Seaducer, Hollywood.*

*Hollywood:* My Sanibel friends Dave Schwerdt and Glenn Pittard named this fly for its flash and style, which they insist gives it a touch of the movie mecca's glitz and glamour. I can't say that its goggle eyes and pearl-white Puglisi flash fiber evoke images of starlets and hot nightspots for me, but it does get the attention of snook.

The Hollywood has a deep profile that effectively mimics deep-bodied baitfish species such as herring and menhaden. It is likely an adaptation of other deep-profile, artificial fiber flies with large plastic eyes, such as a Bay Anchovy. One disadvantage to the Hollywood is its limited durability. Snook's tiny teeth often catch in the wispy fiber strands, tearing them loose and shredding the fly.

*Cockroach:* With its dominant gray, brown, and black hues, the Cockroach loosely mimics a wide selection of crustaceans that snook sometimes eat, but only a handful of dark-colored fish prey species. Some snook anglers who favor this pattern insist that, at night and in dark water, dark flies work best because they are more visible. But in my experience, this is one of those old bromides that have come to be accepted as true mostly through unquestioning repetition. Anyone who takes the time to fish and to observe the extremes of the color spectrum among flies will quickly come to the conclusion that a white, silver-white, or pearl-white fly is more easily spotted in water stained with tannin or roiled and discolored by sand and sediment. And I have caught many snook with white flies on dark nights, as well as in highly discolored water.

*Seaducer:* This is an old-time, tried-and-true attractor pattern. Although cynics may claim that it resembles a red-and-yellow feather duster or a Las Vegas showgirl's costume, it has caught snook for several generations. The Seaducer's broad profile and brilliant colors make it highly visible to both anglers and fish. Its longtime advocates include some of the true legends of saltwater fly fishing, from Lefty Kreh to Charles Waterman. No one I have met has ever claimed that it represents a known prey species, however.

*Soluble Minnow:* There are other glass minnow flies, but this tiny, sparse pattern created by guide Greg Bowdish of Cape Coral, Florida, is a near-perfect imitation of the diminutive baitfish that snook love. In keeping with the scale, it is usually tied on a size 6 hook. Holographic eyes serve as an additional attention-getter. The fact that this fly rides hook-point up helps prevent hang-ups. The Soluble Minnow is particularly deadly when schools of glass minnows are swarming under dock lights at night.

*Everglades Special:* This deep-profile streamer by Enrico Puglisi is intended to imitate a pinfish, one of snook's favorite mini-meals. Green on top and tan with brown stripes beneath, it also has large eyes and a bit of red yarn behind the head to simulate gills. This is the favorite snook fly of Mike McComas, longtime Ten Thousand Islands guide and owner of Lee Island Outfitters in Fort Myers. It is tied with Puglisi's renowned fiber material.

## WEIGHTED STREAMERS

Weighted streamers have two distinct advantages: they get down in deeper water, and when stripped, they work in a jerky, up-and-down action that is highly effective in provoking strikes. This is the same exaggerated, wounded baitfish simulation so favored by spin fishers and bait casters who swear by jigs. Although some fly fishers are loath to admit it, weighted streamers are the jigs of our sport.

*Clouser Minnow:* By far the most popular weighted streamer, and probably the second most famous saltwater fly in the world, Bob Clouser's invention is an indispensable weapon in any snook fly fisher's arsenal. Clousers come in a nearly limitless variety of color combinations, but the most common and popular for snook is the classic chartreuse and white; next is yellow and white, followed by silver and white. All three are baitfish imitations. In the darker colors, such as brown, gray, or gold, Clousers also simulate shrimp and crabs.

The two main disadvantages of the Clouser both have to do with its weight: First, because it lands with a splash, it often spooks snook if cast close to fish in clear water. Second, it puts a hitch in the cast and greater strain on the angler's casting arm than do unweighted flies.

*Woolly Bugger:* In recent years, a number of snook anglers have turned to the old tried-and-true trout streamer tied on larger hooks. Weighted versions are the patterns of choice, especially coneheads and beadheads. A few anglers, including Steve Bailey, one of southwest Florida's top guides, prefer to weight their flies by wrapping the hook shank with lead. This causes the fly to sink more uniformly instead of diving nose first like a jig.

*Crazy Charlie:* This small, sparse pattern is best known as a bonefish fly, but it also works for snook. Like the Clouser, it is really a small jig. It is usually tied and fished to imitate a shrimp or other small crustacean. The most common snook colors are pale pink and pink and white.

*Weighted snook streamers. From top left: chartreuse and white Clouser Minnow, tan and white Clouser, brown and gold Clouser, chartreuse flash Clouser, pink and silver Crazy Charlie, pink and gold Crazy Charlie, Mangrove Crab, Baboon, beadhead Woolly Bugger.*

In sandy areas, the Crazy Charlie is often bumped along the bottom. This technique sometimes works for fussy beach snook. As with other weighted flies in clear water, cast well ahead of the fish—at least 10 to 12 feet—and let it sink. Start the strip when the snook gets within 3 or 4 feet of the fly.

One advantage the Crazy Charlie has over the Clouser is that it is tied with bead-chain eyes instead of the heavier, clunkier dumbbell variety. This makes it easier to cast and stealthier when it lands.

*Mangrove Crab:* This dark brown yarn pattern mimics the crabs that inhabit the branches and foliage overhanging the distinctive marine environment where snook spend a good part of their lives. The logic behind the Mangrove Crab is that the creatures that inspired it sometimes fall into a snook's lair. The crabs' size and comparative vulnerability in the water make them a prized snook snack.

Because it is weighted with small dumbbell eyes, the Mangrove Crab is easier to cast than heavier crab patterns. Its broad body is designed to land with a splat and a splash (not a plop), just like a crab falling into the water. Rubber legs and a fiber tail are good attention-getters for hungry snook. The Mangrove Crab is also deadly for redfish.

*Baboon:* This is another excellent Greg Bowdish creation that he calls a combination shrimp-crab fly; however, it leans heavily toward the crab side. Although it is brighter and flashier than the standard dark brown, it also mimics a Mangrove Crab.

Bowdish ties it in different color schemes, but his preferred pattern is the Fire Tiger version. The body, constructed of stripped copper Mylar tubing, is very distinctive and is accented by a hot orange Polar Fibre tail. For added verisimilitude during a take, Bowdish coats the stripped copper with head cement, giving it a crunchy, crabby feel to a fish that bites down on it.

To help prevent hang-ups in the tangled roots and vegetation, both the standard dark brown Mangrove Crab and the Baboon flies are tied with double weedguards. These paired snippets of 40-pound-test monofilament also add to the realistic feel in a snook's mouth because they prick the fish a bit, like a crab's spiny appendages and exoskeleton.

## SPOON FLIES

Spoon flies were designed to duplicate the wobbling action of the classic spinning and bait casting lures. Most are made of durable composite or plastic-type materials that retain their shape after being chomped on. Many are colored with bright metallic paint, sometimes with metal flakes or metallic foil. A coating of epoxy over the paint or foil adds to the durability factor.

Despite their designation, some spoon flies come in shapes that are a far cry from the soup-sipping utensils they are named for. One of my favorites is the diamond configuration, with split-shot eyes glued to the wing tips to enhance the wobble. This is sometimes called a milk-bottle fly because it can be constructed by clipping out the body forms from plastic milk bottles.

Because most spoon flies are unweighted, have a large surface area for their size, and are often constructed of lightweight plastic materials, they call for an even slower retrieve than streamers to prevent them from riding up on top of the water.

*Spoon flies. From top left: white Milk Bottle Diamond Spoon, gold flake Milk Bottle Diamond Spoon, red and gold Epoxy Spoon, copper foil Epoxy Spoon.*

## POPPERS

Poppers are smaller, lightweight versions of the familiar plugs for conventional tackle. Materials used for their body construction range from high-density Styrofoam to wood, neoprene, and various composites. All these materials have low specific gravities, so the flies float high. Most poppers feature a cone-shaped taper from head to tail. The front of the head—where the hook eye protrudes—is flat, concave, or slotted.

Snook are mainly sight feeders, but with poppers, gurglers, and sliders, extra factors come into play to enhance the flies' fish-attracting qualities: sound vibrations and subtle pressure waves. Both are created by surface disturbances resulting mainly from the contour and size of the fly's head. Although fish have no external ears, their internal hearing apparatus is highly sensitive. And it is a scientific fact that water conducts sound better than air does. One of the most remarkable sensory organs in nature is fishes' lateral lines, which are highly sensitive receptors for detecting pressure waves in their fluid environment. This ability is particularly keen in snook.

In general, the more surface commotion these flies make, the better they attract snook. For this reason, poppers, gurglers, and sliders all call for

*A selection of popper flies in various colors and shapes. Body materials include deer hair, soft rubber, high-density neoprene, and Styrofoam.*

a bit more oomph during the retrieve than the standard streamer strip. Hard, fast tugs are required to create the desired *gloop* sound. As with all retrieves, keep the rod tip pointed at the fly to eliminate slack and sags. If casting in current, mend the line continually to prevent a bow. Longer pulls (12 to 18 inches) also help push as much water as possible. Of the three surface fly types, poppers produce the most dramatic sounds and the most water displacement.

Poppers are highly effective for luring snook out of hiding places deep in the mangroves. In general, the most effective ones land softly when cast and pop loudly when worked. I have not found them to be effective for sight fishing.

Some poppers have no taper, and a few have reverse tapers—thin head and thick tail. These so-called pencil poppers make minimal commotion; there is no real pop, but they dance and bob from side to side when retrieved. Many snook poppers include a clump of bucktail or marabou tied in at the rear end just above the bend in the hook. Effective colors are white, green and white, and red and white.

## GURGLERS

Gurglers are hybrid flies that are most closely related to poppers. With a wide, stubby body and an upward-slanting lip in the front, a gurgler provides three fish-attracting advantages: it is highly visible; it produces the snook-enticing sound denoted by its name; and, when fished correctly, it swims with a slight side-to-side motion when retrieved. Like poppers, gurglers are good for enticing snook out of their ambush lairs. Popular colors are tan and light green.

One effective tactic with both gurglers and poppers is to leave the fly floating motionless for several seconds after casting or between strips. Just as with largemouth and smallmouth bass, the sudden movement of an immobile surface fly can bring a savage strike. Gurglers are generally fished with a slower retrieve than poppers are.

## SLIDERS

Sliders have become very popular in recent years. Like poppers and gurglers, these are surface flies, but unlike the other two categories, sliders are

*Gurgler flies in tan and green.*

not intended to produce distinctive sounds. Instead, they slide through the surface film. Although comparatively noiseless, they are designed to displace significant amounts of water when fished properly, causing a surface disturbance that is sensed by snook as vulnerable prey behavior.

Many of the most popular sliders are tied with large heads of tightly packed deer hair for good flotation and substantial, highly visible silhouettes when seen from below. A significant number are variations on the popular Muddler Minnow freshwater trout fly. Most slider patterns are dark: brown, black, purple.

Going against the dark color tradition, Greg Bowdish has created a hot pink slider with a flat foam head that he calls a Rattlesnake. Its name comes from the tiny rattle tied beneath the head and the action of the tail, a Zonker-style strip of rabbit fur, which shakes and wiggles like a snake during the retrieve.

*Sliders come in a wide variety of colors and styles. Bottom left is the Pink Rattlesnake, a deadly snook fly invented by Greg Bowdish of Cape Coral, Florida.*

# CHAPTER 7

# *At Home in Different Environments*

C hapter 3 laid out snook's general seasonal and environmental patterns: warm months spent in nearshore ocean waters, cool months in protected inshore waters and estuaries. These two main habitat classifications can be broken down into a number of subcategories with their own unique attributes.

In the ocean, snook frequent at least four different environments: areas of structure, including downed trees and other debris, as well as so-called hard-bottom locations where underlying bedrock is exposed; beach shorelines, which are the best places to find cruising summer snook; jetties and piers, both of which provide high-profile structure and cover; and deep passes between barrier islands, where most snook school up to spawn during the warm months. Inshore waters offer even more possibilities: mangrove shorelines, grass flats, oyster bars, bays and bayous, creeks and cuts, large rivers, canals and ditches, and freshwater ponds and lakes.

Successful snook anglers adapt their tactics and techniques to fit the conditions where they are fishing. It is valuable, therefore, to examine the characteristics of the various habitats where linesiders can be found.

## OCEAN HABITATS
### Structure
For devotees of structure, the first task is finding it. Sometimes this is as easy as spotting beachside stumps, trees, or other flotsam and jetsam. Snook love to hide and lurk, and because of the dearth of structure in

most open ocean waters, they often stack up in large numbers wherever they find even minimal cover and camouflage. Cast as close as possible to the debris, but be prepared to force the snook away from it when it hits.

Hard-bottom areas in shallow, nearshore ocean waters can be some of the most productive snook spots anywhere. These rich benthic environments are full of nooks, crannies, and crevices in the rocks—often porous limestone—that attract many snook prey species, both baitfish and crustaceans. They are usually marked by lush seaweed growth that provides even more cover and makes them easy to spot as dark patches on the bottom if water visibility is good. In deeper or turbid water, a boat equipped with a depth finder or fish finder that can distinguish bottom types is a big help in locating hard bottom.

When fishing over hard bottom, make long casts and retrieve the fly over as much of the dark, weedy area as possible. Some hard-bottom areas are configured as narrow strips paralleling the shoreline. If the outer edge is within casting range, cast diagonally out beyond it and strip the fly back over the dark area. Snook often hit when the fly enters the dark zone or as it is exiting on the shoreward side.

Stumps and downed trees are most often found in areas of rapidly changing shoreline contours. Beaches are, after all, "rivers of sand," accreting and eroding at the whims of weather, wind, and tide. Some of the most unstable beaches are along barrier island shorelines, making them likely spots to find sticks and stumps.

Although they can hold good numbers of snook, blowdowns and drowned forests can be very challenging to fish. Sometimes snook may be so far back in the fallen timber and brush that it takes a near-perfect cast to lure them out. Cast tight to the structure, flipping the fly in under trunks and tangles where feasible. When you do hook up, immediately turn the fish's head and force it out into open water. To do this without repeated breakoffs, use a leader with at least a 30-pound-test tippet.

## Beach Shorelines

As previously discussed, sight fishing along beaches in summer is the most exciting kind of snook fishing. It also calls for special tactics. Because snook are among the wariest of fish, stealth is key. Understanding and following a few simple rules will dramatically increase your chance of success.

Do not wade. Many fishermen have difficulty comprehending this, so it is worth repeating. *Do not wade.* Snook sometimes cruise less than a foot

*To have a chance at close-in fish, anglers must stand back from the water's edge.*

from shore in water so shallow that their bellies are scraping bottom and their dorsal fins are creasing the surface. Stay back 10 or 15 feet from the water's edge, and walk parallel with the shoreline.

It is important to constantly scan the water up and down the beach, keeping a sharp eye out for movement. Out of the water, snook are gleaming standouts. And to the uninitiated, it may seem a natural assumption that they would be impossible to miss. But their evanescent coloration provides excellent camouflage when they are in their element, even over a clean, sandy bottom. Many anglers are surprised at how difficult they can be to spot except in the clearest water. Even large snook have a way of sneaking up on a daydreaming angler, especially if they are cruising fast.

The best presentation to cruising fish is a diagonal cast. Put the fly a couple of feet in front of them and strip it away. Never cast over snook from behind and strip the fly back toward them. They will spook every time. As the saying goes: Baitfish do not attack gamefish. Snook know this in their genetic memory.

If you are fishing with a buddy, do not give up on a school if he or she hooks a fish. A quick cast to the pod will often bring another hookup.

About three times out of four, a beach snook will run parallel or diagonal to the shore when hooked. This is a distinct advantage for anglers, especially when fighting big fish, because it enables them to chase the fish down the beach to recover line and prevent being spooled.

### Jetties and Piers
These man-made structures are snook magnets. The reason, of course, is that they provide cover for both snook and their prey. Piers are especially good spots because they offer overhead protection and shade.

When fishing jetties, a long cast parallel to the structure offers the best chance of luring out a fish. Cast as far under piers as possible, working the fly close to pilings. Zero in on sections of water that lie in shadow. The same caveat that applies when fishing other structure is also valid for jetties and piers: try to turn the fish's head immediately and force it out into open water.

### Deep Passes
Fishing large passes often presents a special challenge because of the water depth. Attempt to spot surface fish by looking for nervous water or battered baitfish. I prefer to try a floating line first, but if there is no surface

*When casting to docks and piers, stay well back from the structure, and try to cast as far up under it as possible.*

*When working a mangrove shoreline, stay as far out as you can comfortably cast, and put the fly as close as possible to trunks, branches, and roots.*

action, I switch to an intermediate or full-sink line and a weighted streamer and go deep. Snook can be anywhere in the water column. Often they hit as the fly is stripped up to the surface.

## INSHORE HABITATS
### Mangrove Shorelines

This is snook fishing as most people know it. Almost always done from a boat, it usually involves blind casting to root-tangled margins, although there may be occasional sight fishing in sandy pockets and shallow areas.

When fishing mangrove shorelines, just as when working a trout stream, it is important to learn to read the water and spot likely lies: under overhanging branches, in tidal cuts, deep within dark pockets, and in shoreline indentations. The technique of prospecting with flies is an effective and time-honored method, but on tough days, there can be a lot of casting between fish. And because most mangrove shorelines are shallow, this method is not effective on very low tides. On extreme high tides, it can sometimes be frustrating to hear snook busting bait deep within flooded forests, beyond the range of any cast. The most productive times are the last three hours of the incoming tide and the first three hours of the outgoing tide.

Cast as close as possible to the mangrove roots, and keep the boat at least 40 or 50 feet from the shoreline (the farther out the better) to avoid spooking the fish. Many anglers use a trolling motor to work a shoreline, but a push pole offers more stealth.

Watch and listen for feeding fish. A snook busting bait at the surface makes a very distinctive sound—a *plock* that is a combination of a pop and a hard smack. Once you have heard it a few times you will be able to distinguish it from ladyfish, seatrout, mangrove snapper, and other species.

Remember, patience is a virtue. Take your time when working a particular stretch. Beware of adopting the "grass is greener" attitude, which prompts anglers to fish an area haphazardly and then rush on to the next one, looking for the big fish that they think are just around the bend.

When you do hook a snook, your first concern should be to force it away from the mangroves, because the fish will head for the roots and branches almost every time. Start out down and dirty with the rod, keeping the tip low—even in the water—and pulling horizontally in the direction opposite to the fish's preference. Once you have turned the fish and it is clear of the mangroves, you can raise the tip and fight it conventionally.

Snook love to hide in shady nooks, especially under overhanging branches, but when the water is cold they often change their habits, favoring sheltered, sunny pockets where they can soak up the warming rays.

### Grass Flats

On grass flats, snook can be found cruising for baitfish and crustaceans in the same areas as seatrout and redfish. Sight fishing sometimes comes into play. Look carefully for wakes and signs of nervous water. Occasionally, snook tip down to eat shrimp or crabs, exposing their tails as redfish do. Like reds, they cruise in over the flats on an incoming tide and move back out when it falls. Also, most grass flats are dotted with sandy potholes that draw snook and other fish, especially at the lower end of the tide.

Despite the sometimes very shallow water (6 or 8 inches is enough), snook can be hard to spot in the grass, and they are extremely spooky. When fishing from a boat, be ready to make long casts. The fish can pick up the pressure wave from even a carefully poled boat 30 or 40 yards away. Do not attempt to use a trolling motor. Even this minimal "white noise"

*Watch carefully and step cautiously and quietly when wading grass flats.*

echoes across shallow-water flats like a gunshot in a box canyon. Wade fishers should move slowly and step carefully, trying to avoid crunching shells underfoot or splashing.

## Oyster Bars

Many oyster bars have existed for decades or longer, creating impressive structure masses. These honeycombed accumulations of generations of shells attract baitfish, shrimp, and crabs and, inevitably, the birds and gamefish that prey on them.

Most oyster bars are surrounded by a ring of deeper water—similar to a castle moat—and this is where the snook will be, cruising the edges of the shell heap. Usually these rings have one or two (comparatively) deep pockets where snook also lie in wait. As on the flats, keep an eye out for nervous water, and also watch the wading birds—herons, ibises, egrets, etc. They often pinpoint the greatest concentrations of bait.

Oyster shells can be as sharp as razors and can cut off a leader in a split second. If you hook up, force the fish away from the shell mass.

## Bays and Bayous

These bodies of water are actually brackish water ponds and lakes. They are almost always bordered by mangrove shorelines, and this is where

*Some long-established oyster bars eventually become miniature mangrove keys.*

anglers should focus most of their efforts. But it is also a good idea to prospect holes and channels. Snook generally do not sit in the middle of these deeper areas but prowl the edges and dropoffs, where water depth changes dramatically over a short distance.

Not all bays and bayous are created equal. Water flow, bait numbers, and other factors vary widely, depending on a number of factors. Also, depending on their orientation, the direction of the wind, and the stage of the tide, two bordering bodies of water may have completely different fishing on a given day. If you fail to find action in one, do not assume that the adjacent one will also be fishless.

### Creeks and Cuts

When fished on strong moving tides, creeks and cuts can be extremely productive snook spots. The best fishing is generally on a steep falling tide, when baitfish, shrimp, and other snook foods are swept out of the estuaries.

Tactics for catching snook in creeks and cuts are similar to those used in streamer fishing for trout. Cast down and across the current, letting the fly swing and stripping it back against the current. Slow and easy are the bywords for the retrieve. The current alone usually imparts good movement to the fly. Sometimes it is effective to stop or delay the retrieve, twitching the rod tip occasionally to mimic a baitfish scooting forward and falling back against a strong flow. Even with a slow retrieve, in very swift tidal flows, an unweighted streamer sometimes rides too high. If the fly skips along the surface during the retrieve, switch to a weighted fly or a sinking line.

## Large Rivers

Large rivers, such as the Caloosahatchee in southwest Florida and the Indian River in east-central Florida, are extensive marine ecosystems whose habitat variables are determined largely by the complex interplay between outflowing fresh water from inland regions and tidal salt water from the ocean. These waterways contain elements of many different subenvironments for snook, including mangroves, grass flats, creeks, and bays. The quality of their fisheries is determined by a combination of natural and human factors largely associated with adequate but not excessive water flow and nutrient load.

Especially during the changeover seasons—spring and fall—the mouths and lower reaches of large rivers can offer phenomenal snook fishing. The best fishing is often found in the rich interflow zone, where fresh and salt water mix. These areas move upstream or downstream according to the strength of tidal flows, rainwater runoff, and reservoir releases. Again, snook fly anglers will have the most success by concentrating their efforts on shorelines, structure, and channel edges, not in the middle of large waterways.

## Canals and Ditches

At their best, these generally small waterways mimic the natural habitats of creeks and rivers. At their worst, they are sterile, concrete-lined spillways. Most fall somewhere in between.

Ditches and canals are reliable and often highly productive havens for winter snook. If the water is relatively clear, snook can often be spotted cruising the edges or lying in wait near docks and seawalls. In discolored water, they can be found by watching for bait pods and listening for the sound they make when attacking baitfish on the surface. As in cuts and creeks, the time to fish for snook is on moving tides. Slack-water fishing is nearly always a waste of time.

There is one quirky aspect of canal and ditch snooking that usually does not include catching them. During severe cold snaps, when water

*Ditch and canal fishing, such as here along the Tamiami Canal, is a quirky, intriguing pastime.*

temperatures fall below 60 degrees, semidormant snook—some of them very large—can be spotted beneath docks and boats, suspended and largely immobile. Under these conditions, snook almost never eat. At such times it is best to consider the outing a sightseeing experience and forget about trying to catch them.

Perhaps the best-known canal system for snook fishing is the complex of creeks and drainage ditches along and near the western end of the Tamiami Trail, from Naples, Florida, to the Turner River Canal. Some of my best winter snook fishing has taken place in this area. These intriguing waters, first made famous by legendary fly fishers from Lefty Kreh to Charles Waterman, are easily accessible and have good numbers of snook in winter. The snook numbers dwindle in the summer. Many other species of fish can also be caught, including gar, warmouth, baby tarpon, and largemouth bass.

Two peculiar traits of this fishery are the large numbers of alligators and, in most areas, speeding cars and trucks only a few feet away. Both factors call for an extra measure of caution when fishing. Because of the ditches' proximity to the highway, snook anglers sometimes employ the unusual tactic of car cruising—driving slowly while watching the water for snook busting bait. Lefty Kreh says that he often did it with various fishing buddies in the old days of Everglades ditch fishing.

## Freshwater Ponds and Lakes

Like some other saltwater fish species (e.g., striped bass), snook adapt well to fresh water. They can be found in some surprising places, from golf course water hazards to sweetwater bayous and large lakes. One well-known place where snook are caught is south Florida's Lake Okeechobee, the state's largest freshwater body of water.

Snook get into fresh water in one of three ways. First, they can swim there themselves. They sometimes travel long distances and negotiate mangrove swamps, canals, culverts, creeks, and rivers along the way. In coastal areas, snook have moved into some freshwater ponds and bayous by swimming inland on storm tides that flood areas not normally underwater. Second, some snook get trapped in estuaries that become cut off from the sea by storms and shifting sands. Rain and other freshwater inflows decrease the salinity over time. Third, snook may be transplanted into landlocked waters. The only confirmed transplants I know of were done by anglers, although stories persist (likely fictitious) of fish being dropped in by birds. More than a few fly fishers who live inland have put snook into ponds near their homes so that they can catch them without traveling to salt water.

Because they need strong tidal flows and high salinity levels for successful spawning, snook do not reproduce in fresh water. But once introduced, they can survive for decades.

# CHAPTER 8

# *Snook After Dark*

Because of its distinctive conditions and specialized tactics, snook fishing at night deserves its own chapter. Snook are eager and efficient nocturnal predators. Under the cover of darkness, much of their daytime wariness often disappears. They never become pushovers, but they feed closer in and are less spooky at night.

One of the secrets to after-dark success on snook is the same as at any other time of day: finding them. Structure is always a good bet. Bridges, rocks, and pilings act as snook magnets. So do sunken boats and other jetsam. Narrow channels that funnel tide and baitfish also draw fish.

But the biggest success factor for snook after dark is the contradictory fact that these wary, relentless predators that love to feed on the blackest, moonless nights also are attracted to light. The reason is simple: they go where the food is, and waterside illumination is one of the greatest bait attractors. Light combined with structure—such as lighted docks—makes for some of the sweetest snook spots anywhere.

I have never been enamored of night fishing. Growing up, I chased stripers with my dad on many a Cape Cod summer night, but I always found it aggravating—navigating and fumbling around in the dark, needing a flashlight for the simplest tasks. But fishing under the lights eliminates most of the irritation factors of nighttime angling.

This quirky but intriguing method—often practiced in the spillover illumination of bridges, condos, restaurants, and resorts—does not offer remote, unspoiled settings, but it can be hugely productive. Anyone who has fished under the lights knows what a rush this slam-bang kind of angling can be. It takes place in harbors, bayous, canals, rivers, and passes. Because it usually means casting in toward docks and pilings, night fishing is best done from a boat. A little shore research beforehand can offer clues about the best places to try.

Most docks and waterfront buildings are lighted. "Snook lights"—high-wattage bulbs aimed down at the water—are a common addition to many private docks, but most night snook fishing takes place under incidental lighting. It is both strange and comforting to fish in a neon and sodium-vapor glow. Compared with other night fishing, the logistical details—tying knots, judging distances, boating and releasing fish—are relatively routine. And the brighter the lights, the better. Victor Edwards, who started guiding in the Homosassa area in 1969, calls this kind of snooking "the most consistent technique I've seen. . . . You can develop your own little set of dock lights . . . and if you choose the time of the year, that can be a fairly consistent event."

Night snook fishing is at least partly sight fishing. While methodically working a dock or bridge with blind casts, it is important to keep a watchful eye for big, fast-moving shadows. Also, watch the baitfish. If they suddenly flee or jump in swarms, it means that they are being hunted. As in

*Fishing in the glow of neon is part of the night dock fishing experience.*

mangrove fishing, keep a good distance from the structure, and drift with the wind and current or use a trolling motor for stealth. Some of the best fishing is from the wee hours of the morning until first light.

Like all snook fishing, the best night fishing is on a moving tide— whether incoming or outgoing depends on the area. Anglers should check tide charts and plan their outings accordingly. I have had the best luck on a strong falling tide, which can bring huge shoals of bait moving with it. Dave Gibson, who has guided in the Fort Myers area for eighteen years, has a clear opinion about the best tidal timing: "Number one is a late outgoing tide." Gibson favors new-moon and full-moon tides. Fishing at night on a weak or slack tide is almost always a waste of time.

One advantage of night fishing is that after dark, the normally leader-shy snook are less picky. This means that it is okay to shorten up to 6 or 7 feet instead of the 9 feet or longer that is most advantageous during daylight. Night conditions also allow the use of heavier leaders. Some anglers keep it simple and tie on a piece of straight fluorocarbon, generally 30- or 35-pound test. I prefer to stick with tapered leaders because they lay out better during a cast, especially with unweighted flies. Tippet strength should be at least 15-pound-test, and the bite tippet should be a minimum 30-pound-test.

Gentle fighting methods have no place in dock fishing under the lights. When you get a strike, put on as much pressure as possible to haul the fish out into open water. It takes only a split second for a snook to wrap the line around a piling or cut the leader on a barnacle-encrusted strut. This is one of the few situations when I often choose an 8- or 9-weight rod over my usual 7-weight. The extra backbone provided by a heavier rod can make the difference between landing and losing a big fish.

A few other basic tactics will greatly increase the chances of hookups and landings. As in all other snook fishing, the first rule is to approach the area you plan to fish as stealthily as possible. If you are fishing from a dock, wear sneakers or other quiet footgear, and tread softly. In a boat, start an unpowered drift or switch to a trolling motor, paddles, oars, or push pole at least 100 feet away. Stay as far from your target area as you can accurately cast.

The most promising scenario, of course, is snook tearing into bait. If this happens, cast to that spot as quickly as possible. Try to judge the direction of the fish and put the fly a foot or so in front of it. Often a feeding fish will smash it as soon as it hits the water. But if there is no immediate take, let the fly sink and swing in the current for a second or two, then start the retrieve.

Although spotting snook is the easiest and surest way to locate them, do not ignore places where there are no signs of fish. Remember, they are out of sight below the surface the vast majority of the time, but because of their skull structure and eye placement, snook are usually looking up. If no fish are visible, it is best to cast across the current and let the fly swing down through the lies, stripping slowly.

Like many fish, snook often hold on the down-current side of structure. This way, they expend less energy because they are partly shielded

*Shell and rock shorelines can be excellent nighttime snook spots.*

from the current by pilings, cross-members, seawalls, etc. Also, they can let the food come to them, shooting up to slash through bait as it is swept down into their lies. They also lurk beneath boats of all sizes and far up under docks.

Although the extensive illumination along developed shorelines often provides the most exceptional night fishing, there are also first-rate after-dark opportunities in many unlighted areas—beach shorelines, narrow passes, culvert outflows, and river mouths. Just as under the lights, the key to success is understanding the fish's behavioral patterns. One cardinal rule for night fishing is to always scout out new areas in daylight. This is partly a safety factor. It is easier to determine water depth, the location of obstructions, and other features in daylight.

In summer, the same schools of snook that cruise beach shorelines during the day are also there after dark. As in the daytime, stay out of the water so as not to spook the fish. An additional incentive to remain on dry land is that sharks tend to move in close to shore at night. Walk the water's edge, making diagonal casts and stripping in the fly right up to shore.

Narrow passes, culvert outflows, and river mouths all fish best on outgoing tides, when bait is swept out of estuaries. The merest channels flowing out of the mangroves—seemingly lifeless in daylight—can come alive with bait and snook moving upcurrent with the falling darkness. One evening I fished a shoreline where a small creek flowed out across a wide

*Big snook tend to become less wary under dock lights.*

stretch of sandy shallows. The water over the flats was only a few inches deep, and the channel itself was only 12 to 18 inches. At dusk, the creek outflow was fishless, but as I walked down the shoreline, I made a note of it. An hour later, after dark, I pulled half a dozen small snook out of the mouth of the narrow flow.

Winter, when snook may travel far into the backcountry in search of havens from the cold, is a particularly good time of year for skinny waters and tight quarters, including narrow bridges and culverts. One February, a buddy and I discovered two outflow culverts where, for weeks, we caught snook nearly every night there was an outgoing tide.

Many excellent night fishing spots are accessible only by boat, which can present navigation challenges. Plan to get to your fishing spot before sunset, taking careful note of channel markers and, if appropriate, using your compass and GPS to preplan the return trip. Use marked channels whenever possible, and always make sure that you have adequate lighting equipment, including a high-candlepower spot.

Streamers are generally the flies of choice for after-dark snook fishing, but try top-water patterns—poppers, gurglers, or sliders—if the action is slow. Sometimes the noise and disturbance factors of surface offerings can make for very successful outings.

# CHAPTER 9

# *Finding the Big Ones*

Big snook got that way by being masters of survival. This means that they are not likely to fall for cheap tricks. However, there are ways to increase your chances of catching big fish. Tactics and techniques vary according to the usual factors: season, setting, and time of day.

Remember that most large snook—30 inches or more—are females. As explained in chapter 2, most males transform into females after one or two seasons spawning as males. The evolutionary logic is that larger fish produce more eggs, helping to ensure the species' survival.

## BEACHES

Anyone who has sight fished for snook along the summer beaches has seen these big breeder females. Unlike the smaller males, these fish usually travel singly or in pairs; only rarely do they gather in small pods. Some of these fish are huge—35 inches or more. Sleek but massive, gliding effortlessly through the water, they are magnificent creatures.

During the day, the big females along the beaches generally follow one of two patterns. The first is that, like the smaller male fish, they swim parallel to the shoreline, usually staying farther out and in deeper water than the more numerous males. In this mode they are often on the prowl for prey. The second pattern occurs when they are actively spawning. In this phase they often swim close to shore, attracting retinues of males who tag along, ready to contribute their milt when the females release their eggs.

During these times, all the fish—but especially the big females—are more focused on procreation than on eating.

During the early weeks of summer sight fishing, after a winter spent mainly pounding mangrove roots, grass flats, channels, and potholes with endless numbers of blind casts, it is easy for fly fishers to become mesmerized by the sheer numbers of fish visible. On the best days, schoolie snook seem to come up the shoreline in endless waves—small, medium-size, and massive groupings cruising close in along the beach in an endless piscine procession. But anglers should train themselves not to ignore the water out beyond the ever-oncoming masses of small to medium-size fish. Look for large, moving shadows a foot or two beneath the surface.

One June day, I was having some success catching schoolies 2 to 20 feet from shore, but all the while I was keeping an eye on the water farther out. In the periphery of my vision I spotted a large, dark form moving leisurely from left to right about 50 feet from shore. Because the surface of the Gulf was riffled by a breeze and the shadow was cruising deep, I was unable to distinguish whether it was a single large fish or two schoolies swimming in tandem. I dropped my Schminnow three feet ahead of the dark shape, made one strip, and the shadow shot ahead to grab it. Instantly the answer was clear as the fish headed for Cuba at warp speed, whacking my thumb with the reel handle as it went.

As with most rules, it is occasionally necessary to violate the no-wading imperative for beach sight fishing. One circumstance that dictates getting into the water is spotting a very large fish cruising beyond casting range. If the water is shallow enough, get well ahead of the fish and wade out quickly until you are within comfortable range to put the fly in front of it.

When the big females are in close spawning or actively seeking spawning partners, getting them to take a fly is often a challenge. This is partly because they are distracted by the priority of the reproduction ritual and tend to go off their feed. But it is also because the smaller males that follow and sometimes surround them hit the fly before the big fish can get to it. Sometimes this problem can be solved by making a pinpoint cast within a foot or less of the big fish's nose. If the smaller, trailing males go after it anyway, pull it away from them and make another cast. But because snook attack fast and ferociously, this is not as easy as it sounds. I have caught and released as many as three small males while (futilely) chasing one big female for nearly a quarter mile along the beach. Strangely, the same spawning ennui that causes their disinterest in food also makes them less spooky.

Dawn, dusk, and after dark are good times to find large snook close to shore along beaches. From just before sunset to just after sunrise, lulled by the fading light, they move into areas where schoolies ruled at midday. Keep in mind, though, that while smaller fish cruise blithely over very shallow areas, big fish need and prefer a few more inches of water. Walk the beach during the brightest daylight hours and mark the places where channels cut in close to the beach. When you return to these troughs in low light or darkness, fish them stealthily, staying back a few feet from the water. Remember, even though you cannot spot the cruising snook, their eyes are sensitive enough to detect your movement against a starry or moonlit sky. Also, watch and listen for fish crashing bait, and single out the biggest splashes to cast to.

**OUTFLOW CUTS**

Especially in the cooler months, outflow cuts from bays and bayous can be awesome producers of monster snook. Ideal conditions are a strong

*Large spawning females are usually solitary cruisers.*

*Outflow cuts from bays and bayous can provide spectacular fishing, especially on strong outgoing tides.*

outgoing tide from just before sunset until far into the night. These are the times when big snook move in to prowl dropoffs, flats, potholes, and channel edges. The biggest fish are usually found downcurrent from the mouth of the cut, expending as little energy as possible while waiting for schools of bait to be swept out to them.

Cuts that drain estuaries often form mini-deltas fifty to several hundred yards downstream from their outflows, the result of silt and sediment settling out over time where the flows broaden and slow. These areas of upsloping bottom, shallowing out to sand and grass flats, provide perfect edges for big, cruising snook. This is because the current upsweeping against the shoal bank forces deep-swimming bait toward the surface, making them especially concentrated and vulnerable.

The best way to find big snook in cuts on falling tides is to start at the uptide end and work downstream. If the area is fishable by wading, cast from shore or from the shallowest water possible. With both boat and wade fishing, cast down and across the current, as if you were fishing a river, letting the fly swing and stripping it back slowly, making sure to work dropoffs and channel margins especially thoroughly. These are prime spots to hook up trophy snook. When fishing from a boat, remember to be as quiet as possible, speaking softly and taking care not to bang the hull.

Large fish also move into cuts on incoming tides. But it has been my experience that emptying flows are more productive for big fish by a factor of four or five to one.

## STRUCTURE

Freshwater fly fishers, especially trout anglers, know the importance of structure in finding big fish. For certain highly territorial species, such as brown trout, part of the challenge is deducing where the largest fish will be on a particular stretch of water. The dominant fish invariably seek out the pockets with the best shelter and the most reliable food supply:

*Culvert outflows can transform a strong current into a torrent, setting the water boiling with bait and snook.*

behind a large rock or windfall, under an overhanging bank, or amid a weedy patch. Snook fishing can present analogous situations.

To find big snook in areas with structure, look for the choice lies. Around docks, this is often among or behind the largest grouping of downcurrent pilings. On jetties and breakwaters, the best spots are large pockets between rocks and just off the tip, where the current sweeps and swirls around. Because seawalls are so featureless, any niche or outcropping offers an attractive lair. Unfortunately, areas with blowdowns and stumps can present an unsolvable conundrum. The biggest snook often seek out the tightest, most tangled recesses, presenting little hope for a productive cast and an even smaller probability of landing a fish if it is hooked.

## MANGROVE SHORELINES

When looking for big fish along mangrove shorelines, keep in mind that the trees and their roots are really a complex system of structure. This means that mangrove strategies and tactics are similar to those for docks,

*Dick White of Belfry, Montana, battles a snook hooked near a culvert inflow.*

rocks, walls, and blowdowns. As in these other environments, the most important thing to remember is that the biggest fish take possession of the top lies. In the mangroves, this means the deepest shoreline indentations, the shadiest coves, the water beneath the largest foliage canopies, and the snuggest ambush pockets among the root tangles.

Work the large sites methodically—margins, middle, inner reaches— and do not give up on a spot too soon. It may take several casts to entice a trophy linesider out of its favorite mangrove hidey-hole. Keep a careful eye out for moving water, too. Where there is good tidal flow, there is usually plenty of food. Bruiser snook especially like brushy points jutting out into the current. Also, even the tiniest streams and ditches trickling out of the forest can be big-fish magnets.

# CHAPTER 10

# *Incidental Species*

A big bonus for snook anglers is the many other varieties of fish that are caught—often unintentionally—while pursuing linesiders. It is prudent to be prepared to adapt your tactics and gear to take advantage of these opportunities. The two most common incidental species are redfish and spotted seatrout, but the mix changes according to the areas fished.

It would be normal to assume that, when sight fishing, what you see is what you get. But another adage is even more valid: expect the unexpected. Even in the clearest water, I have pulled reds and seatrout out of the middle of a school of cruising snook. In this run-and-gun style of fishing, it is easy to miss the occasional interloper.

When blind casting, diversity of catch is often the rule, not the exception. This is especially true when fishing where there are large schools of bait on the move. The dream scenario for anglers is gamefish tearing up bait on the surface. In calm water, such a feeding frenzy can be spotted half a mile or more away. These blitzes are also often marked by dive-bombing terns and pelicans. A feeding frenzy can produce an astounding variety of gamefish species. I have often landed three or more different varieties on consecutive hookups. Snook, seatrout, Spanish mackerel, redfish, jack crevalle, ladyfish, bluefish, mangrove snapper, pompano, and even gaff-topsail catfish might be crashing the same bait pod. It is a good idea to carry a few flies with short wire leaders attached to them for the blues and

*Redfish and snook are often found together on grass flats.*

the mackerel. Their piranha-like teeth can slice off even a 30-pound fluo-rocarbon bite tippet in a split second.

The mouths of cuts are also excellent multispecies spots. Snook are not the only fish that know instinctively to wait downcurrent for baitfish and shrimp being swept out of mangrove estuaries on a liquid conveyor belt. Be sure to work the channel thoroughly, from the farthest upstream point to well beyond the end of the outflow, where the water generally shallows out. Snook seem to prefer feeding positions in the upper or mid-dle reaches, while seatrout are often found out over shoals and grass flats, several hundred yards downcurrent. In the deeper water, seatrout will usu-ally be lower in the water column than snook. If you are fishing on or near the surface and getting no action, try switching to a sinking line and/or a weighted fly to get down deep for trout, also known as speckled trout or specks.

As previously explained, the best snook retrieve is slow and method-ical, with short strips and distinct pauses in between. But this is not true for all species. Ladyfish, for example, tear into a fly that is racing through the water. It is almost impossible to strip too fast for them, except for the caveat that streamers should not ride up on top. Anglers should adjust their retrieve according to the species present.

In fresh water and low-salinity areas, snook anglers can find a whole different mix of quarry. One region where this is common is the Tamiami Canal and its connected waterways that drain the Everglades in south Florida. Largemouth bass are the most common fish caught by fly fishers targeting snook in the upper reaches of the system. But warmouths, shell-crackers, Mayan cichlids, gar, and baby tarpon are also present in good numbers. Anglers who find themselves getting many strikes but few hookups should switch to smaller flies. Some of the species' mouths are simply too small to take a standard size 2 snook fly hook. Going down a few sizes to a 6 usually solves the problem.

One family of fish that may be found among snook—sharks—requires a cautionary note. It is not that they are particularly dangerous to hook up on a fly. Frequently, a shark simply cuts off the leader immediately. But if it is hooked in the lip or corner of the jaw, it is possible to land it. I have occasionally caught small bonnetheads, blacktips, and other sharks while pursuing linesiders. It is important, of course, to be careful when unhook-

*Spotted seatrout eat the same flies as snook.*

*In brackish or freshwater canals and ditches, anglers should keep a sharp eye out for alligators, such as these bruisers along the Tamiami Canal.*

ing and releasing them. Use pliers to remove the hook, or clip off the tippet and retie it. It is equally important to take care when releasing snook and other fish if there are sharks in the vicinity. Especially in low light or after dark, do not hold the fish in your hand in the water to revive it. Slip it in quickly, dropping it in nose downward while holding it a few inches above the surface.

# CHAPTER 11

# *A Few Good Places*

Most anglers with a passion for a particular fish species have a favorite place or region they keep going back to. An Atlantic salmon fanatic, like the fish he or she pursues, will return time and again to the Grand Cascapedia or the Spey. For a dedicated steelheader, it may be the Rogue; for a bone fisherman, it might be Christmas Island or Exuma. Likewise, the Big Hole, the Missouri, the Beaverhead, or some obscure stream full of memories may exert a force stronger than gravity on a trout fisherman year in and year out for the better part of a lifetime. Ardent snookers are no exception.

As with other angling pursuits, the allure of a beloved snook fishery may lie in its natural beauty, the number of fish, the size of the fish, the climate, the ambience of the community, or any combination of these and other attributes. For many anglers, the first response that comes to mind when they are asked to pick their favorite snook destination is similar to that of Ray Van Horn, guide and champion angler: "That's a tough one, because I've got so many favorites." When pressed, however, Van Horn commits: "From a pure fly-fishing standpoint, I would have to say the Tarpon Springs, St. Joseph Sound, Honeymoon Island, Anclotte Island beaches in the summer." An important consideration, he says, is "easy access, because you can drive out there and walk the beach, it's public access. . . . I would say it rivals that Sanibel-Captiva area pretty good as far as beach fishing goes."

While Van Horn is a dyed-in-the-wool Gulf coaster, *Shallow Water Angler* managing editor Terry Gibson's snook paradise lies across the peninsula on

*What could be better than being hooked up to a snook with the action backlit by a stunning Gulf of Mexico sunset?*

Florida's Atlantic coast. His favorites include "the coquina reefs and the worm reefs in southeast and east-central Florida. Satellite Beach is great, [as are] Jupiter Island and Vero Beach." He fishes these areas both from shore and from a boat. As for timing, he says, "They really fly fish best in the late spring when the first pulse of greenies (greenbacks) comes in late May." And, as in any area, it is important for anglers to adapt their tactics to the conditions. "It's the exact opposite of you [the southern Gulf coast]," Gibson stresses. "You want low light and some chop. It's not sight fishing at all. You're working the guts and the reefs, the trough between the reef and the beach, the edge of the reef if you can get to it."

For the world's most renowned saltwater fisher, Lefty Kreh, two snook places are close to his heart. "One is the west coast of Florida in May," Kreh says. "There's a migratory run that runs past the Ten Thousand Islands up past Naples. They run about 5 to 12 pounds, really good fish. Another place," he continues, "is Casamar in northeastern Costa Rica on the Rio Colorado." Kreh explains that nearly all the fishing in Casamar is blind casting. "The water's kind of dirty, it's never really crystal clear. But you can catch some really big snook." An interesting twist, he says, is that "there are two kinds of snook; the big ones . . . and there is another run in early January that never gets bigger than 5 or 6 pounds." The huge run of small snook coincides with a massive baitfish influx, when millions of chee-chee, a type of glass minnow, show up at the mouth of the river. Finding the snook is a simple matter of spotting them busting the bait.

"You use a 4-weight rod and little tiny Clousers that are dressed on a number 6 hook," Kreh says. "What I like about it is that you can catch fifty, sixty, seventy, eighty fish on a 4-weight rod and they run anywhere from a pound and a half to three or four pounds."

There is no doubt about my number-one snook fishing area: my home waters around Sanibel Island. With 12 miles of sandy beach on the Gulf of Mexico and many more miles of convoluted mangrove shoreline on Pine Island Sound and the lower Caloosahatchee River, Sanibel presents superb snook fishing in all its myriad permutations. The most awe-

*The author with a 34-inch snook caught on the shoreline of Sanibel Island.*

some, of course, is summer sight fishing along the beaches. This is a world-class experience that easily ranks as one of the most thrilling in all of fly fishing. Another plus about Sanibel is the ambience of the community. Because of its long history of strong environmental stewardship, more than 60 percent of the island is forever protected as public conservation lands and wildlife refuges. Stringent building codes foreclose any possibility of having to face one of the most disheartening angling experiences in many coastal areas: fishing in the shadows of concrete skyscrapers. Also, in sharp contrast to many resort islands, Sanibel's beaches are broad and uncluttered, its estuaries wild and unspoiled, its pace relaxed and sleepy. The hottest nightlife is casting to snook under the dock lights in the east-end canals.

Victor Edwards, a native Floridian who lives in and guides out of Homosassa and Crystal River, lists several places among his favorite snook fishing locations, but he has one that heads the list. "In terms of targeting snook for the average fisherman, the Everglades is almost impossible to beat," Edwards says. When he is down in the 'Glades, Edwards fishes out of Chokoloskee, targeting many of the region's premier waters, including Lost Man's River. Anglers unfamiliar with the bewildering maze of waterways, islands, mangrove forests, and marshes that is the Everglades should always hire a guide. Finding no fish and getting lost are likely outcomes of a blind excursion for beginners. "Venice under the lights" is another favorite snook destination for Edwards, as is "over on the east coast in the Fort Pierce area." Especially productive, he says, is "the intracoastal waterway. . . . [With] a lot of inlets and jetties, they've got a tremendous number of docks over there."

Marshall Cutchin, legendary former Key West guide and publisher of the online fly-fishing magazine *midcurrent.com,* loves the Chokoloskee area as much as Edwards does. "You can go into a place with a johnboat and just know nobody else has been there; maybe not ever, but certainly not in a while," he says. Cutchin's other favorite spot is Whitewater Bay near Flamingo, in the far southern reaches of the Everglades.

# POSTSCRIPT

# A Snook Fishing Ethic

My best fly-fishing pal, Berris "Bear" Samples, has a simple life philosophy: try to leave the world a little bit better than you found it. It is an outlook that we should all try to emulate. And it is particularly relevant to snook fishing.

Half a century ago, like a number of other animal species in the United States, snook faced a real threat of extinction. Fortunately, a significant shift in the national attitude moved the country away from the concept that our natural resources, including wildlife, existed mainly for human exploitation. It was a monumental change that saved the bald eagle, the peregrine falcon, the gray wolf, and the American alligator; it also saved the snook.

For linesiders, the turning point was 1957, when the state of Florida, the most renowned snook destination in the world, banned commercial fishing for the species. Since then, thoughtfully conceived management programs and vigorous enforcement have helped return the Sunshine State to its former status as a world-class snook fishery.

Commitment and vigilance are the only ways to ensure that our children and grandchildren will still be able to pursue this magnificent fish. As individuals, we have little influence, but when we join together, we can change things for the better. A watershed event for snook preservation was the passage of Florida's inshore gill net ban, fought for so hard by the folks at *Florida Sportsman* magazine and the Coastal Conservation Association.

Every snook angler should join at least one angling advocacy organization, as well as one or more environmental watchdog groups that will fight for fishermen and to save fish habitat and clean waters. Worthy organizations include the Federation of Fly Fishers, the Izaak Walton League, the Coastal Conservation Association, the Environmental Defense Fund, Riverwatch, the Natural Resources Defense Council, and the Theodore Roosevelt

Conservation Partnership. These groups and myriad others all work for good causes, although the focuses of their efforts vary.

One thing we can all do as individuals is practice catch and release. Lee Wulff's pronouncement that "a game fish is too valuable to catch only once" is as valid today as when he first said it. This is especially true for snook, which can live as long as two decades. This does not mean that we have to be fanatics. It is okay to eat an occasional snook. I keep about one fish a year and regard preparing and eating the delicious, mild white fillets as a paean to the species. One Thanksgiving I made snook and onion chowder as an appetizer. My wife and I agreed that it was the best fish chowder we had ever eaten.

It should go without saying that the use of barbless hooks goes hand in hand with catch and release. They can make the difference between a simple, safe release and a bloody, fatal injury for a fish that is hooked deep. And there is no reason to lose a snook on a barbless hook as long as you keep the line tight throughout the fight. Also, it is my contention that it is easier to hook a snook, especially in its bony, cartilaginous jaw, when the hook has no barb.

*A good method for reviving snook is the "sucking the thumb" technique.*

*A small snook "getting some air."*

*Gentle is the byword when handling snook.* DAVE FORD

Another important conservation measure is to lay off the fish during times of stress, such as red tide outbreaks, very cold weather (which can kill them), and pollution spills.

If you observe poachers, turn them in. It is cowardice and a moral failure not to. They are stealing from all of us, and threatening the future of our sport. This goes for unscrupulous recreational anglers who keep fish out of season or outside the slot limit, as well as illegal commercial fishermen.

# GLOSSARY

**adult snook**—A snook that has reached sexual and physical maturity. Snook usually reach adulthood when they are between 14 and 19 inches long.

**bite tippet**—A length of heavy leader material tied to the end of a tapered leader. For snook, it is usually 1 foot or less. It may be monofilament or fluorocarbon, with fluorocarbon preferred because of its abrasion resistance. A minimum of 25-pound-test is recommended to prevent snook from cutting through the leader with their sandpaper teeth or razor sharp gill plates.

***Centropomus undecimalis***—The scientific name for the common snook, designated by eighteenth-century German researcher Marcus Elieser Bloch.

**copepods**—Tiny, shrimplike organisms that make up a large portion of the diets of small juvenile snook.

**glass minnow**—Small, slim baitfish with whitish silver, translucent bodies. One of snook's favorite foods, they are commonly seen when fishing summer beaches and under dock lights.

**grass flat**—A shoal area where the bottom—usually a mix of sand, silt, and muck—is grown over with one or more varieties of marine grass. Because grass flats are highly productive for countless baitfish and crustacean species eaten by snook, they are excellent places to find snook, especially on an incoming tide.

**gurgler fly**—A top-water fly usually constructed of foam and feathers. A forward-slanting scoop on the front gives it a wobbling action when retrieved and causes a surface disturbance that attracts snook.

**juvenile snook**—Fish measuring from about $1/2$ inch to 14 inches.

**larval snook**—Generally the first two to three weeks in a snook's life, between the time it hatches from the egg until it is able to swim on its own. Larval snook are free-floating and planktonic, drifting at the mercy of tides and currents.

**leader**—A length (or several lengths knotted together) of clear monofilament or fluorocarbon line attached to the end of a fly line. It is usually tapered from a thick butt end at the fly line to a thin end where it is attached to the bite tippet. For snook, the best length is between 7$\frac{1}{2}$ and 9 feet.

**mangroves**—Several varieties of trees that grow along the margins of saltwater and brackish water estuaries in tropical and subtropical regions. They have extensive and intricate root systems; the root ends are anchored in the substrate, and the rest of the root is exposed within or above the intertidal zone. Mangrove forests are the number-one habitat for snook. Mangroves' geographic range loosely coincides with that of snook.

**outflow cut**—A short opening from one body of water to another. Such places are often excellent for snook fishing when there is a strong tidal flow, and even the narrowest cuts can attract snook.

**oyster bar**—An agglomeration of live oysters and old shells. These are excellent structures for attracting snook prey species and are usually surrounded by a ring of deeper water.

**pinfish**—A deep-bodied, silvery, brown-striped baitfish with sharp dorsal spines. This favorite snook food is found in good numbers in estuarine environments, especially on grass flats and in mangroves.

**piscivorous**—Fish eating.

**plankton**—Microscopic ocean organisms—either animals or plants—that drift freely and are unable to propel themselves. Larval snook are considered plankton, and they also eat other plankton.

**popping fly**—A surface fly, patterned after the popular plugs used by spin fishers, that is designed to create noise and a small splash to attract fish. Common materials used to construct them include Styrofoam, wood, neoprene, and various composites.

**pothole**—A depression in a grass flat. A pothole can often be spotted by its sandy bottom in the midst of a grassy area. Tricks of light refraction and coloration can sometimes make potholes appear shallower than they really are. Potholes range in size from 5 feet in diameter to 30 feet or more.

**protandric hermaphrodite**—A fish that has changed its sex from male to female. With snook, the change generally takes place after a fish has spawned as a male for one or two seasons. Most snook longer than 26 inches are female.

**sight fishing**—Casting to fish that can be seen. Snook can be sight-fished on grass flats, but most sight fishing takes place along beach shore-lines during the summer spawning period.

**spoon fly**—A fly pattern often, but not always, shaped like a spoon. It is designed to wobble when retrieved, but it must be retrieved slowly, or it will ride up on the surface and be ineffective.

**streamer fly**—The most effective and popular type of snook fly. It is a soft pattern constructed of hair, feathers, synthetic materials, or various combinations thereof and designed to swim a few inches below the water's surface.

**stripping basket**—A solid container or mesh basket attached to an angler's waist and used to store line while casting or to strip line into during the retrieve.

**structure**—Any hard, submerged material, including rocky bottom, docks, seawalls, jetties, downed trees and stumps, and vessel wreckage. Both snook and many of their prey species love structure.

**weighted streamer fly**—A type of streamer with weight added to sub-merge it deeper than an unweighted fly; especially useful in channels and passes.

# RESOURCES

**WEB SITES**

Chesapeake Bay Program. www.chesapeakebay.net

Florida Fish and Wildlife Conservation Commission, Fish and Wildlife Research Institute. www.research.MyFWC.com

Smithsonian Marine Station at Fort Pierce. www.sms.si.edu

Smithsonian National Museum of Natural History. www.nmnh.si.edu

Tampa Bay Soundings. www.baysoundings.com

Texas Parks and Wildlife. www.tpwd.state.tx.us

University of Vermont. www.fwie.fw.vt.edu

**PUBLICATIONS**

Muller, Robert G., and Ronald G. Taylor. *The 2002 Stock Assessment Update of Common Snook,* Centropomus undecimalis. St. Petersburg, FL: Fish and Wildlife Conservation Commission, Florida Marine Research Institute, 2002.

# INDEX